DISCOVER

classical music of the

20th Century

by

David McCleery

Published by Naxos Books, an imprint of Naxos Rights International Ltd

www.naxosbooks.com

Printed and bound in China by Leo Paper Group
Design and layout: Hannah Davies, Fruition – Creative Concepts
Literary Editors: Harriet Smith, Ingalo Thomson
Map illustrator: Arthur Ka Wai Jenkins
Timeline: Hugh Griffith

Front cover score extract: The opening of Alban Berg's Violin Concerto

A CIP Record for this book is available from the British Library.

ISBN: 978-1-84379-237-6

Contents

Website

Log onto **www.naxos.com/naxosbooks/discover20thcentury** and hear over two hours of music, all referred to in the text.

To access the website you will need:

ISBN: 9781843792376

Password: Stimmung

website Streamed at 64Kbps to provide good-quality sound.

website Easy links to view and purchase any of the original CDs from which the extracts are taken.

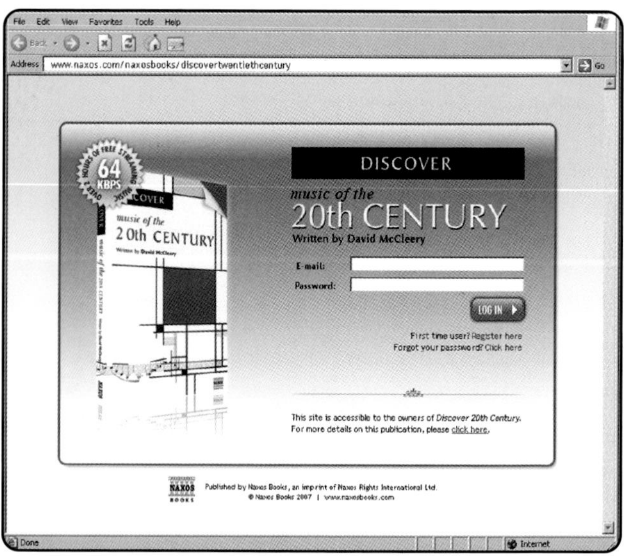

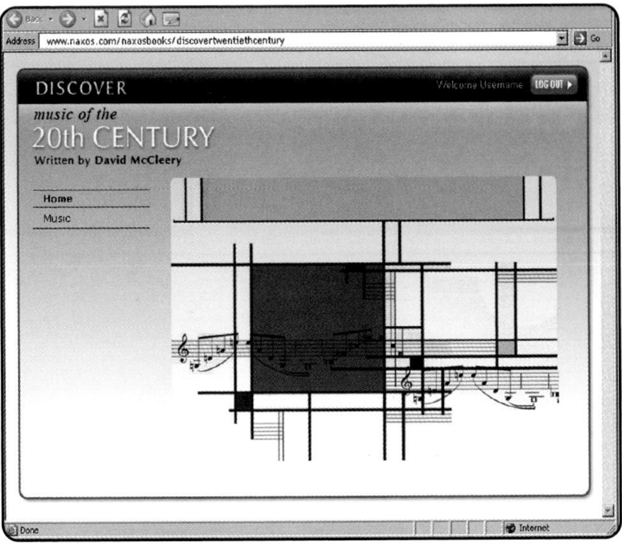

Address www.naxos.com/naxosbooks/discovertwentiethcentury
DISCOVER
Welcome Username
LOG OUT
music of the
20th CENTURY
Written by David McCleery
Home
Music
Done
Internet

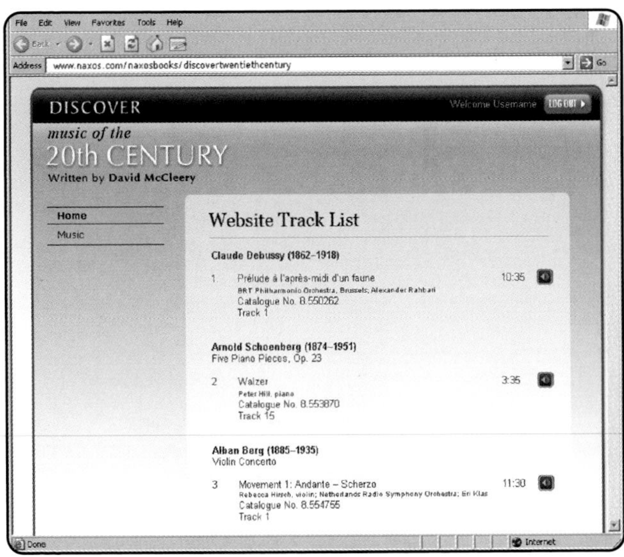

File Edit View Favorites Tools Help
Address www.naxos.com/naxosbooks/discovertwentiethcentury
DISCOVER
Welcome Username
LOG OUT
music of the
20th CENTURY
Written by David McCleery
Home
Music
Website Track List
Claude Debussy (1862–1918)
1 Prélude à l'après-midi d'un faune 10:35
BRT Philharmonic Orchestra, Brussels; Alexander Rahbari
Catalogue No. 8.550262
Track 1
Arnold Schoenberg (1874–1951)
Five Piano Pieces, Op. 23
2 Walzer 3:35
Peter Hill, piano
Catalogue No. 8.553870
Track 15
Alban Berg (1885–1935)
Violin Concerto
3 Movement 1: Andante – Scherzo 11:30
Rebecca Hirsch, violin; Netherlands Radio Symphony Orchestra; Eri Klas
Catalogue No. 8.554755
Track 1
Done
Internet

classical music of the
20th Century

by

David McCleery

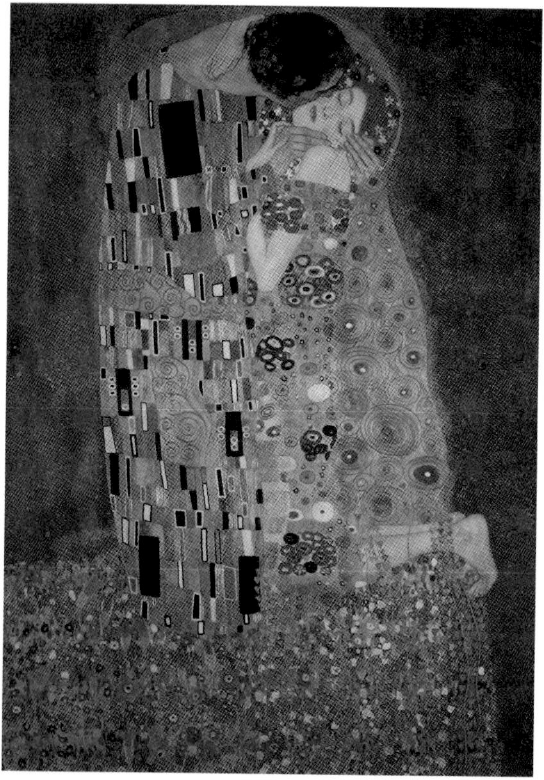

The Kiss, *1908, by Gustav Klimt (1862–1918)*

I. Introduction

Like all great art, great music has always absorbed the spirit and the ideology of its time, expressing them in a way which proves meaningful to future generations. It is impossible to understand the history of twentieth-century music without looking at the events that shaped the world during this turbulent yet exhilarating age. The far-reaching political and mental impact of the two world wars cannot be overestimated: the violent bloodshed of World War I finally came to an end in 1918 with the almost simultaneous resignation of the German Kaiser and the Habsburg Emperor, while in the previous year the Russian revolutions had resulted in the overthrow (and later murder) of Tsar Nicholas II. This dramatically transformed the political map of Europe, with the collapse of the Austro-Hungarian Empire and new, independently ruled nations springing up throughout central Europe. While Communism was established in Russia, political infighting among left and central governments elsewhere in Europe led to Fascist dictatorships in Germany, Spain and Italy. Following the further brutal atrocities of World War II, Europe was divided both physically and ideologically. With the descent of this Iron Curtain between

East and West, the world entered the unstable age of the Cold War – a period of tension and competition between the Soviet Union and the USA and their respective allies that would last until the early 1990s. Music was both directly and indirectly affected by these events in many different ways: certain composers, for example, wrote works inspired by particular events; others were forced by totalitarian governments to write patriotic music in an officially prescribed style.

There were, of course, many other, more positive factors that influenced the course of music in the twentieth century. The amazing speed of technological advancements changed the way in which the world functioned, and opened many new doors for composers. The advent of recording and broadcasting made it easy for everyone to enjoy the sound of a full-size symphony orchestra in the comfort of their own home, hugely increasing the potential audience for music. Recorded media and a faster pace of communications also meant that composers came into contact with, and were influenced by, styles and techniques of other countries, which may otherwise have taken years or even decades to reach them. The development of electronics led experimental composers to create an entirely new style of music after World War II. A fascination with the music and philosophies of non-Western cultures grew from the increased accessibility to remote parts of the world that came with air travel. Throughout the century, new types of music, such as jazz, pop and film music, all made their mark on classical composers and their work.

These diverse factors came to exert their influence on Western classical music at a time when the tradition stood on a threshold. Since the seventeenth century, all music had a firm foundation in tonality, the idea of music being 'in a key'. The pitches of the major and minor scales are organised hierarchically around a key-note or tonic (which gives its name to the key). All the harmonies of a composition are organised around – and gravitate towards – the tonic. But the radical ways in which composers, in particular Richard Wagner, had stretched the system's rules of harmony during the nineteenth century had brought tonality to the brink of collapse. Composers at the outset of the twentieth century had a crisis on their hands: without tonality, how could music possibly have a future? The response to this crisis was a dramatic explosion of creativity: many new and diverse musical techniques and styles appeared, some drawing on the past, and others being invented from scratch. The thread of Western musical development which had progressed in a generally uniform manner for a millennium suddenly splintered off into many independent trends, as different composers each tried to define a future for classical music. There was only one rule left: anything goes.

Change always comes about as a reaction to what has gone before. In the nineteenth century, there had been a reaction against the measured formality of the Classical era. Composers, writers and artists plunged themselves into the depths of the human soul and created works of ever-increasing scale and intensity of emotional expression. However, in the early twentieth century, trends and styles emerged which reacted against this: some composers, particularly those at the cutting edge of new techniques, tended to choose small-scale chamber forms, in stark contrast to the grand Romantic works with huge orchestras and epic durations; serialism, as we shall see, rejected the freedom of form enjoyed by the nineteenth-century composers, returning instead to a formal compositional technique governed by strict rules; and neoclassicism, which had its heyday in the 1920s, superseded self-indulgent emotionalism with a deliberately dispassionate style, possibly expressing a need for escapism following the trauma of World War I.

Much of the music of the twentieth century shocked and confused its audiences; even today, particular dissonant and experimental styles are largely avoided by concert organisers, wary of scaring off the public. But by trying to understand what the composers were aiming for in developing their new techniques, we can approach the music without being intimidated, and can appreciate the wildly diverse creativity which has redefined the music of our times.

II. Pointing the Way Forward

Although Paris had been an important musical centre throughout the nineteenth century, there had been very little distinguished French music since the Baroque era. Conscious of this, a group of composers including Camille Saint-Saëns, Gabriel Fauré and César Franck had founded the Parisian Société Nationale de Musique in 1871. Intending to counteract what they saw as the pervasive and unhealthy influence of Wagner's music, which was laden with chromaticism and dense thematic working, they hoped to encourage a French musical renaissance. The Société did not last beyound the mid-1880s due to internal disputes, but the initiative of its members did act as a catalyst for France to make its indelible mark on twentieth-century music history.

Claude Debussy (1862–1918)

Debussy was the composer responsible for bringing the aims of the Société to fruition, and indeed for introducing the first viable alternative to tonal music. He was born in St-Germain-en-Laye, on the outskirts of Paris, and was accepted into the Paris Conservatoire as a pianist at the age of ten. Regarded as a

Claude Debussy (1862–1918)

"A century of aeroplanes deserves its own music. As there are no precedents, I must create anew."

Debussy, in *La Revue S.I.M.*, 1913

difficult pupil, Debussy was unwilling to adhere to the accepted rules of harmony, and often failed his exams as a result. In 1888 and 1889 he heard Wagner's operas in Bayreuth, and although he was influenced by the way in which Wagner pushed tonality to its limits, he regarded these colossal, mythic music dramas as the end of an old era rather than the beginning of a new one.

Debussy's own music was groundbreaking and, to many, shocking because it didn't seem to have a tonal centre. His *Prélude à l'après midi d'un faune* ('Prelude to the Afternoon of a Faun') website 1 of 1894, for example, opens with a haunting flute melody which meanders ambiguously before developing into a rich, sonorous palette of orchestral colour, creating the effect of floating in the air rather than being rooted in a home key, and only coming to rest at the very end.

Debussy was interested in chords for their colours and sonorities rather than for their role in a continuous harmonic progression. It was this that led to his becoming known as an Impressionist composer (a label he disliked) – his hazy and colour-based musical style seeming to have parallels with the Impressionist paintings from the 1870s and 1880s by Monet, Manet and Degas. Many of Debussy's works from the early years of the twentieth century have evocative, Impressionistic titles, such as *Reflets dans l'eau* ('Reflections in the Water') and *La Fille aux cheveux de lin* ('The Girl with the Flaxen Hair'); these were not meant to have any specific programmatic meaning, but they created a mood associated with the visual image. In 1889 he had been greatly impressed upon hearing Javanese gamelan music at the Universal Exhibition in Paris. This fed his desire to find alternatives to the major and minor scales of traditional harmony, such as the harmonically ambiguous whole-tone scale (in which the scale is broken up into six equal steps) and the exotic-sounding pentatonic scale (a five-note scale, represented by the black notes of a piano, which is common in folk idioms around the world). The piano prelude *Voiles* ('Sails') from 1910 is almost exclusively based on the whole-tone scale, while the pentatonic scale formed the basis of many of the melodies in his 1905 orchestral masterpiece *La Mer* ('The Sea').

Debussy not only re-established a strong musical tradition in France, but, by shifting the weight of compositional focus from traditional harmonic progression to chordal and orchestral colour, he showed that there were ways forward for music which didn't rely on strict tonality. His music was challenging to the ears of his day, requiring audiences to listen in a new, unfamiliar way, and as a result it often received bad reviews from the critics. But his example resonated throughout Europe, and he proved to be a major influence on such diverse figures as Ravel, Messiaen, Stravinsky and Bartók.

Debussy wrote his *Prélude à l'après-midi d'un faune* to accompany a reading of the lengthy and dense poem of the same name by Stéphane Mallarmé. In a letter to his friend Georges Jean-Aubry dated 25 March 1910, Debussy describes playing the piece through to Mallarmé prior to the first performance:

'...Mallarmé arrived looking like a soothsayer, with a Scotch plaid over his shoulders. He listened, and then there was a long silence before he said: "I wasn't expecting anything like that! This music prolongs the emotion of my poem and conjures up the scenery more vividly than any colour."

After the first performance he sent me a copy of *L'après-midi d'un faune* inscribed with these lines:

If you would know with what harmonious notes
Your flute resounds, O sylvan deity,
Then hearken to the light that shall be breathed
Thereinto by Debussy's magic art.

A document of prime importance, for anyone who's interested.

In any case, it's my happiest memory of a period when I wasn't yet plagued by "Debussysme".

Yours,

C.D.'

III. Post-Romanticism

The Romantic era didn't end all of a sudden. Although Debussy began composing in a new style in the 1890s, there were plenty of composers who continued to write music inspired by the Romantic aesthetic until well into the twentieth century. The term 'post-Romanticism' is rather vague and open to interpretation; it refers to music which extends the language of the Romantic era, without actually breaking away from its ideals.

Richard Strauss (1864–1949)

The German composer Richard Strauss took the already heightened emotionalism of Romantic music and intensified it to such a degree that it became more decadent than passionate. His music was an early example of the developing artistic style known as Expressionism, which became very popular in Europe after 1905 among visual artists such as Wassily Kandinsky, George Grosz and Edvard Munch and composers such as **Arnold Schoenberg** (1874–1951) and **Alban Berg** (1885–1935). Between 1886 and 1898, Strauss wrote a series of eight tone poems

Richard Strauss (1864–1949)

"I cannot bear the tragedy of the present time. I want to create joy."

R. Strauss, quoted in Derek Watson, *Music Quotations*, 1924

(a symphonic work usually in one movement, inspired by a non-musical idea such as a poem or a painting). In *Don Juan* (1888–9) and *Till Eulenspiegel* (1895) there is an irrepressible flamboyance and exuberance, which escalates into epic and often dissonant decadence in *Also sprach Zarathustra* (1896) and *Ein Heldenleben* (1898). As the new century began, Strauss turned his attention to opera, and his burgeoning Expressionism reached towards the realms of violence and eroticism. *Salome* (1905), based on the play by Oscar Wilde, closes with a highly disturbing scene in which the heroine attains a state of sexual frenzy when she is brought the severed head of John the Baptist on a platter. In *Elektra* (1908), after Sophocles' tragedy, Strauss depicted – within a tale of murderous obsession in the ultimate of dysfunctional families – some of the most vile characters ever encountered in opera.

The debauched nature of Strauss's Expressionist music is prophetic of the gradual rise of Fascism in Germany in the first half of the twentieth century. However, Strauss himself was deeply affected by the direction in which his country was moving. Although he attracted criticism for not making more of a public stand against the Nazis, he did make some personal sacrifice for his principles: he refused to denounce the Jewish writer Stefan Zweig and lost his official job as President of the state music organisation, the Reichsmusikkammer. One of his last works, *Metamorphosen* (1945), written when he had reverted to a lush, less dissonant post-Romantic style, is the deeply moving elegy of a man heartbroken by the depravity, betrayal and devastation of World War II.

Elsewhere in Europe in the last decades of the nineteenth century, a number of countries with relatively low musical profiles (not least Britain) produced composers who went on to establish a national music tradition, inspiring generations of younger composers to build upon it. Often the styles of these composers is best described as post-Romantic rather than 'modern', possibly because the relative isolation of their countries denied them easy access to the cutting-edge innovations occurring on mainland Europe.

Sir Edward Elgar (1857–1934)

"The secret of happiness for an artist when he grows old is to have a passion that can take the place of his art."

Elgar, quoted in *The Gramophone,* 1957

After the death of Henry Purcell in 1695, England had boasted no composers of real international importance before the emergence of Elgar in the 1890s. As a composer and musician, he was largely self-taught. His father ran a music shop in Worcester and as a boy Elgar took the opportunity to teach himself a wide variety of instruments. Throughout the 1880s and 1890s he developed his craft by writing pieces for local amateur organisations. Although early works such as the overture *Froissart* (1890) are characteristic of his mature style, it was not until towards the end of the century that his masterly *Enigma Variations* (1898–99) ensured that his reputation spread first to London, and then internationally. We tend to regard Elgar's music as quintessentially English, its noble quality mirroring our own impressions of Edwardian England. Yet in many of his works, such as the two symphonies of 1908 and 1913, there is an inner passion beneath the stateliness, more understated than in most late-Romantic music but just as powerful. During World War I Elgar's state of mind underwent a significant change, which was reflected in his extraordinarily poignant Cello Concerto of 1919. With the death of his beloved wife Alice the following year, he lost much of his creative spirit and wrote little for the remaining fourteen years of his life. But by that stage he had already triggered a renaissance in British music, inspiring a whole generation of composers and ensuring that Britain would play an important role in the history of twentieth-century music.

Scandinavia

Jean Sibelius (1865–1957)
Carl Nielsen (1865–1931)
Further north, in Scandinavia, Jean Sibelius and Carl Nielsen, both born in the same year, heralded the beginning of a rich new era of musical creativity in their respective countries.

> ***"Give me the loneliness either of the Finnish forest, or of a big city."***
> Sibelius, quoted in Layton, *Sibelius,* 1965

Sibelius's music established an international profile for a specifically Finnish tradition. Since 1809 Finland had been a

Grand Duchy of Imperial Russia; Swedish was the official language of the country (Russian rule having been preceded by a long period of Swedish dominance), and the Finnish-speaking majority resented their political and cultural repression. Sibelius scored his first major public success with the choral symphony *Kullervo* (1892). Like many works written throughout his career, it was based on the Finnish national epic poem, the *Kalevala*, and stirred strong nationalist feelings among the Finnish people. The authorities, nervous of the powerful effect of such patriotic music, went so far as to ban the public from whistling tunes from Sibelius's symphonic poem *Finlandia* following its premiere in 1899.

It is for his seven symphonies that Sibelius is particularly revered; and rightly so, for they are among the greatest of the twentieth century. His mature style grew out of the Romanticism of Tchaikovsky (whose influence is evident in the Symphony No. 1 of 1899), and is characterised by mysterious, sinewy tunes (such as the majestic brass tune in the finale of Symphony No. 5) as well as a feeling of expansiveness, evocative of the isolated lakes and forests of the Finnish landscape. A diagnosis of throat cancer in 1908 brought Sibelius face to face with his own mortality. Although he recovered, his Symphony No. 4 (1911) marked a new darkening of mood in his music. As he got older he became more reclusive; at the same time his musical gestures became more economical and his structures more condensed, which added an intensity of expression to his sound-world. His final symphony, No. 7 of 1924, is a mere twenty minutes long, but so much was packed into its single-movement span that it has an epic quality.

With his growing reclusiveness and the paring down of his style, the rate of his creative output slowed down in a manner similar to that of Elgar; although he lived for another thirty years, he published only a small handful of minor works after 1927.

> ***"There is hope for the new generation if it will work from within and not seek originality in externals, biding its time like the mother who carries the fruit of her womb within her until the great day dawns."***
>
> Nielsen, quoted in *Living Music,* 1925

Though their music was stylistically quite different, there are similarities between the careers of Sibelius and his Danish contemporary, Carl Nielsen. Nielsen likewise set new standards for Danish music, and his catalogue of works is also dominated by a great cycle of symphonies, which progressed almost simultaneously with those of Sibelius, though in a different direction. Nielsen was born into a very poor family on the island of Funen. Music was in the family blood: his mother sang folksongs to him to send him to sleep as a young child, and his father was a well-known folk violin player. So from an early age he developed a strong affinity with Danish traditional music, which would later emerge in his songs, his chamber music and particularly in his cantata *Springtime on Funen* (1922) – a romantic idyll recalling the happy days of his childhood. He won a scholarship in 1890 to travel to Germany where he heard the music of Brahms and Wagner, each of whom represented the opposite poles of contemporary musical thought. While impressed by Wagner's operas, Nielsen found the incessant leitmotifs (recurring musical phrases attached to a particular character or theme) rather absurd and his early symphonies show instead a strong Brahmsian influence.

In contrast to Sibelius's symphonies, which became increasingly internalised, Nielsen faced confrontation head-on as his style developed. In the final movement of the Symphony No. 4 (1914–16), subtitled 'The Inextinguishable', there is a dramatic on-stage battle as two sets of timpani challenge each other for supremacy. The appearance of a lyrical theme from the first movement resolves the conflict, representing the inextinguishable nature of the 'will of life', which Nielsen perceived as the essence of the work.
A similar but more modernist effect is heard in his Fifth Symphony, completed in 1922, when an extremely disruptive improvised side-drum break threatens – but ultimately fails – to obliterate the musical texture. For Nielsen, this passage represented a battle between good and evil – a subject prominent in everyone's mind so soon after the Great War. His sixth and final symphony, the 'Sinfonia semplice', was written in 1924–5. It is a fascinating and mysterious work, ironic and playful but underpinned by a strange sense of spiritual awareness.

IV. Serialism and Twelve-Note Music

While Debussy had taken some steps away from tonality, other composers took a more radical approach and, in the first twenty years of the new century, totally abandoned it. A new generation of composers was producing loud, dissonant and wildly rhythmic music which frequently shocked and dismayed its audiences. On top of that, there had been the unprecedented horrors of World War I: to many it must have seemed as if the world had gone mad. No doubt these factors contributed to a sense of disillusionment which caused composers like Elgar and Sibelius to retire from composition in the 1920s.

In an effort to bring some order to the chaos, **Arnold Schoenberg** (1874–1951) invented a brand new method of composition variously referred to as serial, twelve-note or dodecaphonic music – a system which could totally (but didn't necessarily have to) replace tonality as a basis for music. Schoenberg and two of his Vienna-based pupils, **Alban Berg** (1885–1935) and **Anton Webern** (1883–1945), were the main protagonists of this new style in the 1920s and 1930s. Collectively they are referred to as the Second Viennese School.

The traditional major and minor scales, upon which tonal music had been based for three centuries, split the octave into seven steps – a mixture of whole steps (tones) and half steps (semitones). Within these scales some notes have greater significance than others, the most important of them being the key-note or tonic (next in importance is the note located five steps above it, called the dominant). In Schoenberg's new method, however, each of the twelve half steps (semitones) was given equal status. With no hierarchy among the notes, there could no longer be any sense of a home key.

Under this system the composer would use all twelve notes, arranging them into a row, or series. The notes, however, had to be heard in the same order throughout the piece. The rhythm could change, as could the dynamics, and several of the notes could be played simultaneously – but the order was sacrosanct. It was also possible to play around with the series in other ways, such as playing it back to front (retrograde) or upside down (inverted).

This might sound like a rather dry method of composition, and indeed this criticism has often been levelled against twelve-note technique. But it did offer an entirely new way of thinking, and was arguably the most influential musical innovation of the century. Certain compositional devices of the past, such as the fugue, had also had a mathematical basis, and the challenge was for a composer to create something stimulating and beautiful within the given set of rules.

Arnold Schoenberg (1874–1951)
Schoenberg was born in Vienna to Jewish parents. As a child he studied violin and cello but didn't embark on any formal compositional training until the age of nineteen, when he befriended and became a student of the composer Alexander Zemlinsky (whose sister Schoenberg was to marry in 1901).

Schoenberg, like so many composers in the late nineteenth century, fell under the spell of Wagner's music. His *Verklärte Nacht* ('Transfigured Night') – a string sextet from 1899 – is pure late-Romanticism, full of ravishing textures and harmonies, and it clearly draws on Wagner's chromatic musical language – a far cry from the atonal music for which Schoenberg is best known. But, like Debussy, Schoenberg felt that Wagner's music represented the end of tonality without offering an alternative way forward, and he became determined to establish a new musical starting point for the twentieth century. His music became Expressionistic in style, demonstrated in the dreamlike and dissonant *Erwartung* (1909) for soprano and orchestra, and in the ground-breaking *Pierrot lunaire* (1912). The latter is for female voice and quintet, and the voice has to deliver the text in a way that is half-sung, half-spoken, with only an approximation of pitch (*Sprechgesang*). Schoenberg's Expressionist music of this time is now usually described as being 'atonal': tonality as the gravitational force had disintegrated, with consonance no longer differentiated from dissonance. In 1909 Schoenberg wrote his Three Piano Pieces, which as his Op. 11 were the first fully atonal pieces of music to be published.

Abandoning tonality as a foundation for composition was a major step towards forging a new musical language, but still

Schoenberg felt that the total freedom of atonality wasn't sufficiently rigid to provide an inner logic to his music. Between 1912 and 1923 he wrote very few works, dedicating his time instead to developing the twelve-note technique which would provide him with the framework he needed for atonal composition. The fruition of all this work can be found in the last of his Five Piano Pieces, Op. 23 website 2 – a Waltz. It is based strictly on a twelve-note row, but the listener should not try to hear where the row starts and stops; the serial construction is more a framework within which the composer can work than a device to help the listener appreciate the piece. Listen instead to the rhythmic gestures at the opening of the Waltz (which are heard again with greater clarity from 0′50″–0′52″) and the spiky semiquavers from 0′25″–0′27″. You can hear the former rhythmic gesture between 0′21″–0′23″, 0′44″–0′55″ and 1′29″–1′41″; and the spiky semiquavers at 0′33″–0′40″, 1′24″–1′28″ and 2′33″–2′42″. These are just a few examples of where these gestures appear, and in fact the whole Waltz is derived from these two motifs, which Schoenberg repeats and develops in imaginative ways, creating an unusual piece of delicate sophistication. It is no surprise that reactions to such a revolutionary type of music were mixed. In 1928 the audience at the premiere of Schoenberg's Variations for Orchestra – his greatest twelve-note work for orchestra – expressed such strong outrage that the concert nearly had to be stopped.

Although he had adopted the Lutheran faith in 1898, Schoenberg's Jewish heritage caused him problems when the Nazis came to power, and he was obliged to give up his teaching post at the Academy of Arts in Berlin. In 1933, the widening of anti-Semitic legislation forced him to leave Germany altogether. After short spells in Paris (where he converted back to Judaism) and Boston, he finally settled in Los Angeles, where he accepted a position at the University of California. Many of his works from the American years sound less radical than his earlier twelve-note works. The Chamber Symphony No. 2 (1939) recalls the rich Romantic harmonies of *Verklärte Nacht,* and in other works, such as the Piano Concerto (1942), he incorporates some tonal elements within the twelve-note technique.

Alban Berg (1885–1935)

It is often thought that the composers of the Second Viennese School strode forward into the realms of atonality, totally disregarding the past. However, in the case of Alban Berg, this is far from the truth. Although he enthusiastically adopted the twelve-note technique, he managed to combine it with a rich, late-Romantic Expressionism and, in some cases, blatant and unashamed tonality. In Berg's works, we can often hear the influence of his older compatriot Mahler, whose epic works were an important bridge between Romantic and twentieth-century music, and who was one of Berg's particular heroes.

Like Schoenberg, Berg had little in the way of musical education until he was nineteen and enrolled in the older man's composition classes. Before then, he had confined himself mainly to writing songs in a late-Romantic style, and the voice remained a potent inspiration to him throughout his

Alban Berg (1885–1935)

"The best music always results from the ecstasies of logic."

Berg, quoted in *The New York Times* magazine, 1975

career. During six years' study with Schoenberg, Berg's style matured greatly, and he absorbed much of his teacher's fascination with atonality without losing his love of lyricism and Expressionism: in 1915 his first major orchestral work, Three Pieces for Orchestra, Op. 6, was described by his pupil Theodor Adorno as like an amalgamation of a Mahler symphony and Schoenberg's Orchestral Pieces, Op. 16.

The *Lyric Suite* (1926) was Berg's first large-scale work in which he used Schoenberg's recently invented twelve-note technique. Despite its atonality, it is an extremely expressive and emotional work, and it was not until long after his death that the discovery of some letters to a woman named Hanna Fuchs-Robettin revealed a hidden programme within the work. It became clear that he had been passionately in love with Mrs Fuchs for much of his life, and the *Lyric Suite* had been a eulogy to her. Berg was fascinated by the symbolism of numbers, and in many of his works he represented himself by the number 23 and Hanna Fuchs by the number 10. Both these numbers crop up in many guises within the *Lyric Suite,* be it tempos, number of bars in a section or the length of movements. The work also contains a quotation from Wagner's *Tristan und Isolde,* perhaps a suggestion from the composer that the love between him and Hanna Fuchs, like the lovers in the opera, could only be fulfilled in death.

Berg spent much of the last six years of his life working on his second opera *Lulu* (his first, the Expressionist masterpiece *Wozzeck,* is widely acknowledged as one of the greatest operas of the twentieth century). However, in April 1935, Manon Gropius – the nineteen-year-old daughter of Mahler's widow Alma and her second husband, and a close family friend of Berg's – died of polio. Berg was so affected by her death that he interrupted work on the opera to write a Violin Concerto website 3 dedicated 'to the memory of an angel'. The work is in two movements, each split into two sections. The first movement is a depiction of Manon's life, and the second describes her death and transfiguration. It is a twelve-note work, based on a single tone row (which is clearly heard on the solo violin between 1′00″–1′10″) but arranged in such a way as to give a strong feeling of tonality (at 0′50″, for example, the music seems to be rooted in G minor). The second section of the first movement (beginning at 4′24″) is dance-like, representing Manon's joyous spirit, and in parts is reminiscent of a Ländler from a Mahler symphony. It is not just a tribute to the life of Manon Gropius – there are other meanings hidden in this work. Berg quotes a Carinthian folk-tune (heard on the solo violin at 10′07″) which may be a veiled reference to a Carinthian servant girl by whom he fathered an illegitimate daughter when he was seventeen. Berg also weaves the numbers 10 and 23 into the whole structure, again alluding to his love for Hanna Fuchs.

Shortly after completing the Violin Concerto, Berg contracted septicaemia when an insect sting became infected. He died on Christmas Eve 1935, before the concerto was premiered. The third act of *Lulu* also remained unfinished, and his widow Hélène refused to allow anyone access to the sketches during her lifetime. It was not until 1979, after Hélène's death, that the work was completed (using Erwin Stein's earlier vocal score for Act III, the orchestration prepared by Friedrich Cerha) and premiered in its entirety.

Anton Webern (1883–1945)

"Music is natural law as related to the sense of hearing."

Webern, in *The Path to the New Music,* translated 1963

Anton Webern (1883–1945)
During his lifetime, Webern was the least famous of the Second Viennese School composers, and his music was rarely heard in public. Yet just shortly after his death, his imaginative use of twelve-note technique led Boulez to describe him as the very threshold to the future of music.

After becoming disillusioned with his compositional studies first at Vienna University and then with Hans Pfitzner, Webern found in Schoenberg his ideal teacher and followed his principles rigorously. A few of Webern's early works are tonal, such as his orchestral *Passacaglia*, Op. 1 (1908). But after this point, every work he wrote was atonal, and after 1924 exclusively twelve-note. This was in contrast to Berg, and even Schoenberg in his later years, both of whom took a freer approach. But even though Webern's music is governed by rigid systems, it has an expressive quality that shows his deeply spiritual side and his love of nature. To him, the mathematical basis of his musical structures mirrored the natural perfection of the ice crystals and the flowers he encountered when hiking in the Alps. His comment to Berg that all his music after the *Passacaglia* related to the death of his mother, and the pregnancy of his daughter being a direct inspiration for his String Quartet, Op. 28 (1938), show that a wealth of human emotion underlies all his music.

Webern's music is constructed from the variation and repetition of tiny motifs or gestures, which lends the music an air of mystery and spiritual awareness. All the gestures stand in isolation from each other but collectively they create a broader canvas of sound, a style known as musical pointillism. It refers back to painters such as Georges Seurat and Henri-Edmond Cross at the turn of the century who created secondary colours not by mixing paint, but by juxtaposing tiny dots of primary colour. Reacting to Webern's Six Bagatelles for string quartet (1913), which collectively last a mere four minutes, Schoenberg marvelled at how he had achieved the musical equivalent of expressing 'an entire novel in a single gesture'. Webern's Five Pieces for chamber orchestra, Op. 10 website 4-8, written in 1910, give an excellent example of his concise but intense style. The third piece is the longest at just 01′44″ while the others last between 30 and just over 60 seconds each; yet the work feels mysteriously substantial, despite its brevity. In the first piece, Webern's pointillist technique is evident in the way he dots his musical canvas with tiny gestures on individual instruments to create a magically shifting kaleidoscope of colours and textures.

Webern's life was cut tragically short in the aftermath of World War II. On a visit to his daughter in Mittersill on 15 September 1945, he stepped outside to smoke a cigar. He was accidentally shot and killed by an American soldier, who mistook him for an associate of his black-marketeering son-in-law. Webern left a very small body of work: he assigned opus numbers to only thirty-one pieces, none of which lasts longer than ten minutes. He would never have guessed that his posthumous reputation would rank him among the most influential musicians of the century.

V. Neoclassicism

We have already seen a variety of ways in which composers attempted to move music forward at the outset of the twentieth century. And towards the end of the second decade, a new movement arose which took its inspiration from the practices of, in particular, the eighteenth century. Neoclassicism, which was to blossom in the 1920s and 1930s, was a reaction against the unfettered emotionalism of Romantic music, and a return to the gestural restraint and compositional techniques of music from the Baroque and Classical eras. Paris was at the heart of the neoclassical movement (unsurprisingly given that France was keen to break free from the powerful influence of the Austro-Germanic tradition and establish a musical identity of its own), but neoclassicism was by no means limited to within the borders of France: the Russian composer **Sergey Prokofiev**'s Symphony No. 1 'Classical' (1917), a delightful work which sounds like Haydn updated to the twentieth century, was one of the first pieces that was regarded as neoclassical; and in Germany **Paul Hindemith** (1895–1963) was another leading protagonist of neoclassicism.

Les Six

It was a group of composers known as 'Les Six' – **Georges Auric** (1899–1983), **Louis Durey** (1888–1979), **Arthur Honegger** (1892–1955), **Darius Milhaud** (1892–1974), **Francis Poulenc** (1899–1963) and **Germaine Tailleferre** (1892–1983) – that was largely responsible for establishing Paris as the centre of neoclassicism. Their association was a loose-knit one which began in around 1916 and was based on their mutual friendship and an irreverent attitude towards Romanticism and Impressionism. They were championed by the writer Jean Cocteau, and their musical aesthetic was inspired by the eccentric composer **Erik Satie** (1866–1925). Satie's strange, and sometimes beautiful, works tended towards the absurd, with titles such as *Genuine Flabby Preludes (for a dog)* and *Bureaucratic Sonatina*. Satie's surrealism deliberately promoted emotional detachment and had an ironic quality that influenced not only Les Six but also neoclassical music as a whole. The influence of jazz, which in the second decade of the century was becoming popular in Europe, is also heard in much of their music. Jazz of course was nothing to do with the eighteenth century but its clarity of style and its texture represented a rejection of Romantic and Impressionist qualities which was one of the tenets of neoclassicism.

But the camaraderie of these six composers was not to last. In 1921, Durey withdrew from a ballet called *Les Mariés de la Tour Eiffel* which had been intended as a collaborative project. This caused bad feeling, particularly with Cocteau who had provided the scenario for the ballet, and Les Six disbanded soon afterwards. But they had already sown the seeds of musical neoclassicism in Paris. After the split, the various members went their own separate ways: Durey joined the Communist party and dedicated himself to writing music for socialist causes; Milhaud embraced Viennese Expressionism; Tailleferre continued to compose throughout her life, though most of her work remained unpublished until after her death; Auric became a prolific and successful composer of film scores in France, Britain and the USA; and Honegger's music grew darker and more troubled as he became increasingly disillusioned, particularly after World War II.

"Above all, do not analyse my music. Love it."
Poulenc, quoted in Pierre Bernac, *Francis Poulenc*, 1977

Of all the members of Les Six, Poulenc had been the joker of the pack. But in spite of his seemingly frivolous nature, he was ultimately the most successful. The *Trois Mouvements perpétuels* (1918), Suite in C (1920), both for solo piano, and the Diaghilev ballet *Les Biches* (1924) are typical of his neoclassical style. Although he never totally abandoned his sense of wit, Poulenc began to display a deeper and more serious side to his character soon after the disbanding of Les Six. Following the death of a close friend in the 1930s he rediscovered his Roman Catholic faith and wrote a series of powerful religious choral works including *Litanies à la Vierge noire* ('Litanies to the Black Virgin', 1936) and the Mass in G (1937). It was when writing for voices that Poulenc was at his very finest. From 1935, he embarked upon a lifelong friendship and artistic collaboration with the baritone Pierre Bernac, and for twenty-five years they performed recitals together, with Poulenc writing a large number of songs specifically for Bernac. He wrote his first opera *Les Mamelles de Tirésias* ('The Breasts of Tirésias') in 1944. It is a comic work to a surrealist text by Guillaume Apollinaire which reminds us that, despite the increased gravitas of his work, Poulenc's sense of humour remained intact (the story tells of a married couple who change sex and produce 40,000 children). Nevertheless, he went on to write two more operas of a very different nature: *Les Dialogues des Carmélites* ('Dialogues of the Carmelites', 1957) is an entirely serious and deeply moving drama about the persecution and martyrdom of the Carmelite nuns during the French Revolution; and *La Voix humaine* ('The Human Voice', 1959), for a single female singer and orchestra, is a sharply drawn psychological portrait of a jilted woman and her increasing state of despair as she talks on the phone to her lover.

Poulenc's attitude to his own work was modest and realistic. He was quite happy to admit that he was not a musical innovator, saying, 'I think there's room for new music which doesn't mind using other people's chords'. But while he may not have been a revolutionary, there's no question that much of his music, his songs and chamber music in particular, ranks among the finest of the century.

Maurice Ravel (1875–1937)

The other major French figure of the early twentieth century was Maurice Ravel. Comparisons are often made between his music and that of Debussy. It's true that there are similarities

Maurice Ravel (1875–1937)

"I think and feel in sounds."

Ravel, quoted in Jules Renard, *Journal*, 1907

in terms of their sonorous harmonies and their interest in exoticism and Impressionistic techniques, but fundamentally they are quite different: Ravel's music is essentially tonal, whereas Debussy uses different scales to avoid the feeling of a home key; Ravel's rhythms and structures have a Classical precision, while Debussy's tends to be more irregular and vague.

As Ravel was growing up, Debussy, thirteen years his senior, dominated the French music scene and it would have been almost impossible to escape his influence entirely. Ravel himself acknowledged that he did learn much from Debussy, but cited Fauré (with whom he studied at the Paris Conservatoire for six years), Chabrier and Satie as more important influences.

Impressionism and Orientalism, as well as the influence of Spanish culture (his mother was Basque), can be found in Ravel's early works, such as *Pavane pour une infante défunte* ('Pavane for a Dead Princess', 1899), *Rapsodie espagnole* (1907) and the song cycle *Schéhérazade* (1903). In 1909 the impresario Serge Diaghilev commissioned him to write a score for his company the Ballets Russes, *Daphnis et Chloé*, and through his connection with the company he become friends with Igor Stravinsky, who was working simultaneously on *The Rite of Spring* (discussed below).

Around the beginning of World War I, Ravel began to move towards a more neoclassical style. In his piano piece *Le Tombeau de Couperin* ('Homage to Couperin', 1917) website 9, he honoured the composer François Couperin (1668–1733) by writing a suite using dance forms of the Baroque era – a Prelude, Fugue, Forlane, Rigaudon, Menuet and Toccata. The third movement, the Forlane, is based on a graceful dance form that originated in northern Italy.

Like so many composers based in Paris around that time, Ravel came to adopt a jazz idiom in some of his later works, including the blues-inspired slow movement of the Violin Sonata (1927) and the Piano Concerto for Left Hand (1930). (This concerto was written for the pianist Paul Wittgenstein who had lost his right arm while serving in the Austrian army during World War I.) But despite his growing interest in modern types of music such as jazz, Ravel remained true to his neoclassical principles. His Piano Concerto in G (1931) – this one for both hands – also contains some elements of jazz within a Classically structured framework, which Ravel said owed much to Mozart.

Whether Ravel was writing for piano, chamber ensembles or symphony orchestra, there's a great range of colour and sonority which is immediately recognisable. He often conceived his music at the piano and subsequently orchestrated it; many of his works exist in both solo piano and orchestral forms. In 1922 he also orchestrated Mussorgsky's *Pictures at an Exhibition,* written originally for piano in 1874, and it is Ravel's version that is most commonly heard today.

From 1932, Ravel suffered chronic ill-health due to an organic brain disease, the first signs of which had appeared seven or eight years earlier. The disease slowly eroded his creative abilities and his nervous system; in the last year of his life his speech was badly affected, and he couldn't even sign his name. In December 1937 he underwent surgery, but died just a few days after the operation.

Igor Stravinsky (1882–1971)

Stravinsky was one of the towering figures of twentieth-century music. He enjoyed a long career, with a number of distinct stylistic phases. Stravinsky may not have invented any brand new techniques in the way that Schoenberg did, but the startling originality of his works, coupled with his fresh emphasis on an irregular but powerful rhythmic drive, has influenced music ever since.

He was born near St Petersburg, where his father was a distinguished bass in the Imperial Opera. On the advice of his parents, he went to university to study law, but it was not long before he changed direction, being taken on as a private pupil by the great composer Nikolay Rimsky-Korsakov (whose son was a fellow law student). Another lucky break ensued in 1909 when the impresario Diaghilev heard and was impressed by some of Stravinsky's works. This was to lead to one of the most important artistic collaborations of the century. Stravinsky moved to Paris and over the next four years Diaghilev commissioned him to write three scores for the Ballets Russes. These were characterised by their modernist musical language which combined exotic orchestral colour, biting dissonance, driving rhythms and Russian folksong. *The Firebird* (1910) was the first work to be produced, followed in 1911 by *Petrushka* website 10-11. The character of Petrushka is the Russian equivalent of the clown Pierrot, and the story tells of his unhappy life at a Russian fairground under a cruel master. The bustling opening section, 'Shrovetide Fair' was eloquently described by the musicologist Roman Vlad as sounding 'like a gigantic accordion or a broken-down fairground organ'. The insistent flute tune heard at the opening

Igor Stravinsky (1882–1971)

"My music is best understood by children and animals."

Stravinsky, quoted in *The Observer*, 1961

represents the cries of the street vendors, and at 0′19″ the lower strings introduce snatches of a melody based on a Russian folk-tune, *The Song of the Volochobniki*, on which the rest of the section is based (the tune is heard clearly at 1′13″). Stravinsky's third Diaghilev ballet, *The Rite of Spring* (1913), proved to be one of the most revolutionary works of the century. The subject matter – the sacrifice of a young girl as part of a pagan ritual – together with the violent rhythms and atonality within the score shocked the audience at the premiere and a riot broke out. There was so much commotion that the dancers couldn't hear the music, and Diaghilev had to stand in the wings, shouting directions.

With the arrival of war, Stravinsky's music took on a new direction; as can be heard in pieces such as *The Soldier's Tale* (1918) and the Three Pieces for Clarinet (1919), he started working on a smaller scale, and discovered jazz for the first time. This general scaling-down of his musical style represents the early stages of Stravinsky's neoclassical phase, which was to last almost thirty years. He took a less lyrical approach to this new style than did his French friend, Ravel. Stravinsky's first post-war score for the Ballets Russes (which had disbanded for the duration of the war) was *Pulcinella* website 12 (1920). One of the best-known of all neoclassical works, it gives an imaginative twentieth-century thirst to music attributed to the early-eighteenth-century composer Giovanni Pergolesi. Towards the end of the work, there is a short section titled 'Vivo'. The music is clearly based on Baroque material, but the intentionally clumsy-sounding orchestration, with its trombone slides and solo double bass, adds an irony that could only belong to the twentieth century.

The premiere of Stravinsky's ballet *The Rite of Spring* on 29 May 1913 at the Théâtre des Champs-Elysées in Paris famously caused a riot. Writing in the *Chronicle*, Stravinsky later described his impressions of the evening:

'I have refrained from describing the scandal which it evoked; that has already been too much discussed. The complexity of my score had demanded a great number of rehearsals, which Monteux had conducted with his usual skill and attention. As for the actual performance, I am not in a position to judge, as I left the auditorium at the first bars of the prelude, which had at once evoked derisive laughter. I was disgusted. These demonstrations, at first isolated, soon became general, provoking counter-demonstrations, and very quickly developed into a terrific uproar. During the whole performance I was at Nijinsky's side in the wings. He was standing on a chair, screaming "sixteen, seventeen, eighteen" – and they had their own method of counting to keep time. Naturally the poor dancers could hear nothing by reason of the row in the auditorium and the sound of their own dance steps. I had to hold Nijinsky by his clothes for he was furious and ready to dash on to the stage at any moment and create a scandal. Diaghilev kept ordering the electricians to turn the lights on or off, hoping in that way to put a stop to the noise. That is all I can remember about that first performance. Oddly enough at the dress rehearsal, to which we had, as usual, invited a number of actors, painters, musicians, writers and the most cultured representatives of society, everything had gone off peacefully and I was very far from expecting such an outburst.'

Just before World War II, both Stravinsky's mother and his wife died; he moved to Hollywood where he married Vera de Bosset, with whom he had been in love for twenty years. Despite the success of his works, Stravinsky's income was modest and he hoped he would be able to increase his earnings by writing music for the movies. However, it is a very different discipline from that of writing for the concert hall: quite the opposite of having total structural and expressive freedom, composing film music involves providing precisely timed music cues and evoking a mood predetermined by the director. This discipline suits some composers better than others and Stravinsky's efforts in this direction were unsuccessful.

In 1948 he wrote his only full-length opera *The Rake's Progress*, to a libretto by W.H. Auden. It was one of his last neoclassical works, and shortly afterwards he shocked the musical establishment by adopting Schoenberg's twelve-note technique, thereby entering the final fifteen-year phase of his creative life. The two composers had in fact been near neighbours in California, but they never met as each considered the other's aesthetic to be the antithesis of his own, and they thought they would have nothing in common. By the time Stravinsky began to write twelve-note music, its inventor had died. Stravinsky's twelve-note music, such as *Canticum Sacrum* (1956) and *Threni* (1968), though less accessible – and much less performed – than his earlier works, has a gravitas and eloquence that can be very rewarding. Stravinsky died in New York on 6 April 1971; according to his wishes, his body was transferred to Italy and buried on the Venetian island of San Michele near his friend and collaborator Diaghilev, who had died in 1929.

VI. An English Musical Renaissance

The mighty example set by Elgar heralded a new age of musical creativity in England. Between 1872 and 1913, there were born the five outstanding international figures of Vaughan Williams, Holst, Walton, Britten and Tippett. There was also a wealth of figures who are slightly less familiar today but who played a vital role in helping to define a new national style, among them **Gerald Finzi** (1901–1956), **Peter Warlock** (1894–1930) and **George Butterworth** (1885–1916).

This new style is often referred to as the pastoral style. It is typified by rich, luscious orchestral sounds and tonal harmonies which call to mind the rolling hills and fields of the English countryside. It was also influenced by a new interest in English folksong, initiated by the research of **Cecil Sharp** (1859–1924). Composers such as Vaughan Williams and Butterworth travelled around Britain, collecting and transcribing traditional folksongs, and using the modal flavour of their discoveries to colour their music. **Gustav Holst** (1874–1934) was another figure who was fascinated by the folk-music movement and he often joined Vaughan Williams on his song-collecting field trips. Holst, however, was less inclined than some of his colleagues to absorb the sound of traditional music into his own work, and many of his pieces, particularly those from the early part of his career, were more influenced by the grandeur and chromaticism of Wagner. Although his monumental orchestral suite *The Planets,* premiered in 1918, is one of the most frequently performed pieces of twentieth-century music, Holst didn't receive proper recognition for it in his lifetime; and even today, the remainder of his output is relatively rarely heard. He wrote many works for amateur organisations, such as the children's choirs and orchestras at the London schools where he taught for most of his life. He also had a strong interest in the East and wrote several works inspired by Indian tradition, including the opera *Savitri* (1909; based on a story from the ancient Indian epic, the *Mahabharata*) and the four sets of *Choral Hymns from the Rig Veda* (1908–12), the texts of which he translated himself from Sanskrit into English.

"I seriously advise all sensitive composers to die at the age of thirty-seven. I know I've gone through the first halcyon period, and am just about ripe for my critical damnation."

Walton, quoted in *The New York Times,* 1939

Although the English composers who emerged in the first thirty or forty years of the twentieth century cultivated their own highly imaginative and individual styles, few were radicals in the same vein as Stravinsky or Schoenberg. In his early career, the Lancashire-born composer **William Walton** (1902–1983) gained a reputation as a modernist *enfant terrible* on the British music scene. He started to compose as an undergraduate at Oxford University, and it was while there that he met the poet Sacheverell Sitwell. Sitwell's family took the young Walton under its wing and supported him as an 'adopted brother' for ten years, until he was earning enough through his music to support himself. It was an eccentric and bohemian family, and through the Sitwells Walton met many of the leading literary figures of the day. As a lodger in their family home from 1920, he lived in an environment of progressive artistic ideas which was reflected in early works such as the atonal String Quartet (1920–22) and the anti-Romantic, often spiky *Façade* (1922) – a setting for reciter and six instruments of nonsense poems by Sacheverell's sister, Edith Sitwell, which called to mind the frivolity of 1920s Paris. However, with the premiere of the Viola Concerto in 1929, it became apparent that Walton was abandoning modernism to develop instead his own post-Romantic language that grew out of the Elgarian tradition.

Walton's mature style is heard at its best in his powerful oratorio *Belshazzar's Feast* (1931) and the First Symphony (1935) as well as in a number of the masterly scores he wrote for films directed by Laurence Olivier, notably *Henry V*, *Richard III* and *Hamlet*. By the middle of the century, the gathering momentum of the avant-garde movement made Walton's music unfashionable. This, coupled with the poor reception of his opera *Troilus and Cressida* in 1954, caused him great disappointment and resulted in a significant decrease in his compositional output. He spent most of the rest of his life on the beautiful island of Ischia just off the coast of Naples, where he had moved with his wife in 1951.

Ralph Vaughan Williams (1872–1958)
Like Walton, Vaughan Williams also found himself out of fashion in the 1950s, but this time due to the social and political disillusionment of post-war Britain. The very 'English' sound of his idiom was thought to represent the no-longer relevant values of the Imperial age, and what was once acclaimed as pastoral style was now written off as 'cow pat music'. However, his is a highly personal musical language – deeply felt, often passionate, sometimes dark and brooding, and much more than just a proud expression of nationalism. While Vaughan Williams's style was profoundly affected by his extensive knowledge of folksongs, which he began collecting in 1902, as well as his love of English Tudor music, he was also a composer with a truly international outlook. After studies in Berlin with Max Bruch in 1897, he felt that his musical textures still needed refining and in 1908 travelled to Paris for lessons with Ravel to 'add a bit of French polish' into the mix.

It was after his studies in France that he considered himself to have found his true voice, and some of his first great works, including *Fantasia on a Theme of Thomas Tallis* and the song cycle *A Shropshire Lad,* appeared between 1908 and 1910. At the same time, he embarked upon his cycle of nine symphonies. The second of these, subtitled 'A London Symphony', was written in 1913 but subsequently dedicated to the memory of his fellow composer and friend George Butterworth who was killed in the Battle of the Somme. Although there are specific London references in the symphony, such as the chimes of Big Ben in the first movement and the depiction of hansom cabs in the second,

Ralph Vaughan Williams (1872–1958)

"What we want in England is real music, even if it only be a music hall song. Provided it possesses real feeling and real life, it will be worth all the off-scourings of the classics in the world."

Vaughan Williams, quoted in *The Vocalist,* 1902

Vaughan Williams didn't intend it as programme music. He suggested that the listener should think of it as a symphony 'by a Londoner' (even though he had been born in a small village in the Gloucestershire countryside) rather than one that set out to tell a specific story about the city. His Symphony No. 3 'Pastoral' website 13 appeared in 1922. It was conceived when Vaughan Williams was serving in France during World War I, and although its style, as the subtitle suggests, is characteristic of English music of the time it also has a sense of intense pain and yearning – an outlet for the composer's emotional reaction to the war. The third movement has a typically folk-like feel, particularly at the opening and the trumpet tune heard at 1′53″. However, there are no folk-tunes in this work, and Vaughan Williams rarely made direct use of traditional material in his music. Instead, he absorbed the rhythm and atmosphere of folksongs and let them colour his own work, thus building a new and original tradition out of the old one. His Symphony No. 4 (1934) marked a departure towards a more harsh and dissonant style which became a common feature of his later symphonies (although he returned to pastoralism in the Fifth).

Vaughan Williams composed in almost every musical genre. In addition to orchestral works and chamber music, he wrote a vast quantity of choral music and songs. In his seventies, he started to write film scores, completing eleven between 1940 and 1957. His most famous score was for *Scott of the Antarctic* (1948), the musical material of which formed the basis of his Seventh Symphony *Sinfonia antartica.* Throughout his life he also devoted much energy to writing for the stage, with five operas, five ballets and several other 'stage spectacles'. Although his dramatic works have enjoyed only limited success, a number of his operas, in particular *The Pilgrim's Progress* (completed in 1951), contain some of his finest music. Despite increasing deafness, Vaughan Williams continued to compose until shortly before his death, from a heart attack, on 26 August 1958.

Benjamin Britten (1913–1976)

Britten, arguably the greatest English composer of his generation, transformed the musical life of his country in many ways. He injected a new lease of life into its operatic tradition; he founded the internationally renowned Aldeburgh Festival in the Suffolk countryside in 1948, and converted the malt house in nearby Snape into one of Europe's finest concert halls; he also redefined music education in Britain by creating a body of works for children which accommodated the limitations of young performers without resorting to a patronising idiom. His music achieved greater international popularity than that of his older colleagues, whose style was sometimes considered too specifically English by orchestras abroad.

Precociously talented as a child, Britten began to compose at the age of five. He was never attracted to the English pastoral style, and, although essentially a tonal composer throughout his career, he was more interested in the musical developments on mainland Europe than in his own country. This attitude caused problems for him when he studied at London's Royal College of Music; his teachers there, after awarding him a travel scholarship, banned him

Benjamin Britten (1913–1976)

"Night and silence – these are two of the things I cherish most."

Britten, quoted in Christopher Headington, *Britten,* 1981

from studying with Berg – whom Britten revered – as they associated Berg's radicalism with artistic degeneracy.

After graduating from college, Britten spent four years writing music for documentaries at the GPO Film Unit where he became friends with W.H. Auden, who was employed there as a poet. When Auden went to America in 1939 with the writer Christopher Isherwood, Britten followed them a few months later with the tenor Peter Pears, who was to become his lifelong partner. The unique sound of Pears's voice was central to the conception of many of Britten's operas and songs, and theirs was one of the most fruitful and productive partnerships in the history of music. (The sexual nature of their relationship remained publicly unacknowledged until after Britten's death.) Notable works from the American years include the masterly Violin Concerto (1939); the *Sinfonia da Requiem* (1940), an expression of his anti-war feelings and dedicated to the memory of his parents; and his first opera *Paul Bunyan* (1941).

Britten and Pears returned to England in 1942 and set up home near the remote fishing village of Aldeburgh, not far from where Britten had been born. There he started work on *Peter Grimes,* one of the greatest operas in the English language. It is the story of a gruff fisherman whose emotional repression is directed aggressively towards his young apprentice, who later dies in a tragic accident. Grimes's condemnation by the local community leads to false accusations of murder and eventually to his own suicide. The ideas of the outsider and the corruption of innocence crop up frequently in Britten's works, particularly in the operas, and they were central to the composer's own psychological make-up. The sense of musical isolation he felt

The premiere of Britten's opera *Peter Grimes* on 7 June 1945 at London's Sadler's Wells theatre marked the beginning of a new era in British opera. The following extract from an article by 'a Critic' in *The New Statesman* in summer 1945 shows just how talked-about an event it was:

'I can vouch for the truth of the following incidents on a single-track bus journey last Saturday. They seem almost to amount to proof that we are becoming a nation of high-brows. A friend boarded a 58 bus at Green Park, asked the conductor whether he went past Sadler's Wells. "Yes, I should say I do," he replied. "I wish I could go inside instead. That will be threepence for *Peter Grimes*." All the way to Rosebery Avenue, a young man sitting next to my friend whistled the Tarantella from Walton's *Façade*; it is not an easy tune to whistle and the whistler did *not* get off at Sadler's Wells. But my friend did, and as he left the bus he heard the conductor shouting at the top of a loud voice: "Sadler's Wells! Anyone else for Peter Grimes, the sadistic fisherman!"'

at college combined with his homosexuality cast him, in his own mind, in the role of the eternal outsider. His paternal love for children and his love for the purity of the unbroken voice reflect how much he valued the innocence of childhood. Subsequent operas, including *Albert Herring* (1947), *The Turn of the Screw* (1954) and *Death in Venice* (1973), explore these issues in different ways. (In the case of *Albert Herring,* corruption has a positive effect when the eponymous young hero, having won twenty-five pounds for his moral purity, blows his prize money on a wild night out, gaining self-confidence and a valuable dose of life experience as a result.)

In addition to his fifteen operas, Britten wrote an enormous number of songs and choral music. One of his most popular choral works, *Hymn to St Cecilia* website 14, sets a poem by W.H. Auden – an ode to the patron saint of music, whose Feast Day falls, coincidentally, on Britten's birthday, 22 November. In this work, completed on the boat journey back from America in 1942, slick key changes and the rhythm of the words are used to give the piece a dynamic momentum, the compositional techniques hidden beneath textures of such beauty and clarity that the music sounds effortless.

Composers were increasingly interested in non-Western cultures as the century progressed, and Britten was no exception. The colourful score of his ballet *The Prince of the Pagodas* (1956) is heavily influenced by the sound of the gamelan which Britten had heard while on holiday in Bali; the stylised music and dramatic pacing of *Curlew River* (1964) – the first of his three church parables – was based on the Japanese Noh drama *Sumidagawa,* which he had seen in Tokyo eight years earlier.

Britten's health began to deteriorate in the 1970s and his rate of composition slowed down as he found it increasingly difficult to work. By late 1976 it was clear that he was slowly but surely fading away. In a letter written at the end of November, Pears described to a friend how Britten was 'calm and clear and ready to go'. He died a few days later, on 4 December.

Michael Tippett (1905–1998)

"I like to think of composing as a physical business. I compose at the piano and like to feel involved in my work with my hands."

Tippett, quoted in Murray Schafer,
British Composers in Interview, 1963

Another seminal composer to emerge in the first half of the twentieth century was Sir Michael Tippett. Musically speaking, he was a late developer and after achieving only mediocre results during his initial time at the Royal College of Music in London between 1923 and 1926, he embarked on a career as a French teacher. However, he indulged his inner drive to continue composing, which led to an increasing awareness of certain flaws in his technique, and in 1930 he decided to return to the Royal College where he remained for two years.

The 1930s were a time of personal discovery for Tippett. Politically, he formed strongly socialist beliefs after a period of time in the north of England, where he had seen for the first time the levels of poverty endured by many of his fellow countrymen. In addition, world events in the run-up to World War II clashed with his deep-seated pacifist ideology (in 1943 he was jailed for three months as a conscientious objector). He was also coming to terms with his homosexuality. A course of Jungian dream therapy helped him to work through these issues, all of which became absorbed into his psyche as he moved towards resolving his personal crises, and influenced his music for years to come. It was at this point that he felt he had unlocked his true voice as a composer and he pointed to the second movement of his String Quartet No. 1 – directly inspired by the experience of falling in love for the first time – as a turning point in his career.

Many of Tippett's works from the 1930s to the 1950s were neoclassical in conception. The Concerto for Double String Orchestra (1939) uses a language derived from the English pastoral style within the framework of the concerto grosso – a genre popular in the Baroque era. *A Child of Our Time* (1939–41), one of the greatest oratorios of the twentieth century, was modelled on Handel's *Messiah* and the Passions of J.S. Bach. It was conceived following Kristallnacht – the horrific German pogrom of 9 November 1938 – as a lament on the suffering of the oppressed. Tippett had a magpie-like approach to composition and here he widened his message, alluding to the suffering of the black Americans by using negro spirituals within the work.

In 1947, inspired by the success of Britten's *Peter Grimes,* Tippett started working on *The Midsummer Marriage,* the first of his five operas. It's a life-affirming work whose plot is a typically eclectic amalgam of ideas based on Jungian concepts, Indian mythology, Mozart's *The Magic Flute* and the *I Ching,* as well as the writings of T.S. Eliot, Shaw and Aristophanes. The musical language is bright and exuberant, full of breezy harmonies and delicate orchestration that call to mind his Vivaldi-inspired Symphony No. 2 (1957).

Tippett's operas may be seen as the backbone of his compositional output. From the theme of love in *The Midsummer Marriage,* he turned to war in his second opera, *King Priam* (1961), which heralded his move towards a more complex and modernist language. *The Knot Garden* (1970) is a candid exploration of modern psychological and sexual issues, and his last two operas, *The Ice Break* (1976) and *New Year* (1988), comment on the troubles faced by contemporary society, divided as it is by race and generation.

Even in his mid-eighties, Tippett had lost none of his fascination with new types of music, and in *New Year* he incorporated rap and reggae into the score. Despite his preoccupation with dark subject matter, many of his late works – *New Year* included – are imbued with exuberance and the sense of hope for a better future. He died in 1998, just days after his ninety-third birthday. The catalogue of works that he left represents an eloquent legacy of one individual's quest to find beauty and meaning amid the brutalities of the modern world.

VII. Nationalist Music

The nationalist movement in music emerged in around 1860. It grew out of a desire to express resistance against domination by foreign powers and was particularly strong in Eastern European nations such as Bohemia (now the Czech Republic), which formed part of the Austro-Hungarian Empire. By borrowing from traditional songs and folklore, composers created works which provided a focus for a nation's pride in its own culture and which, as we've seen in the case of Sibelius, could have a sufficiently powerful and popular effect to instil fear in governments. Although the political need for such music declined as more and more nations achieved independence, the interest in folk culture persisted. In the twentieth century, folksongs were a useful tool in helping to establish a national style in countries where there wasn't much by way of a living musical tradition. Vaughan Williams's research into folk music had a strong melodic and harmonic effect on English music in the first half of the twentieth century. Sibelius's expansive textures, although directly inspired by traditional music only rarely, were strongly evocative of the Finnish landscape. They were built upon by the composers who followed him, including

Aulis Sallinen (b. 1935), who has often drawn inspiration from Finnish history and folklore. This is notable in his powerful opera *Kullervo* (1988) which is based, like Sibelius's work of the same name, on the national epic, the *Kalevala*. Spain was another country with an extremely low musical profile until the twentieth century, when **Manuel de Falla** (1876–1946) established an unmistakably Spanish classical music idiom. It is coloured by the rhythms and melodies of traditional music, in particular Andalusian flamenco.

In Eastern Europe, the interest in using folk material remained strong among composers well into the twentieth century. Stravinsky used traditional Russian songs in his early works, including *Petrushka* and *The Rite of Spring*. The music of Czech composer **Leoš Janáček** (1854–1928) is often characterised by brief, irregular phrases which are a distinctive feature of the folksongs of Moravia (the eastern part of the modern-day Czech Republic). This can be heard in the fourth movement of his *Sinfonietta* website 15, written two years before his death in 1928. And from the early 1900s the composers **Béla Bartók** (1881–1945) and **Zoltán Kodály** (1882–1967) jointly undertook extensive research on Hungarian folk music which had a profound effect on their own music. The typically Hungarian flavour of the suite from Kodály's 1926 folk opera *Háry János* and his *Dances of Galánta* (1933) is accentuated by the highly conspicuous and exotic sound of the cimbalom – a traditional Hungarian instrument.

Ironically, while the use of folksong in classical music initially symbolised a move towards political freedom, it became a sign of political and artistic repression in the music

Leoš Janáček (1854–1928)

of the generation of Eastern European composers born in the first decades of the twentieth century. Some governments in the Eastern bloc demanded that composers write popular and rousing nationalistic music to encourage a sense of loyalty from the impoverished peasantry.

Major figures such as **György Ligeti** (1923–2006), born in Transylvania just before the area was lost by Hungary to Romania, and the Poles **Witold Lutosławski** (1913–1994) and **Krzysztof Penderecki** (b. 1933) found themselves obliged to write folk-based music until the late 1950s, when the easing of political restrictions enabled them to join their Western colleagues in exploring the radical new techniques of the avant garde. Although Lutosławski claimed towards the end of his life that he had never felt under any pressure to write in a particular way, when his Symphony No. 1 was banned in 1949 by the Stalinist authorities as too 'formalist' he developed a fresh, tonal style. It was often based on traditional Polish melodies, as witnessed in his *Little Suite* (1950) and Concerto for Orchestra (1950–54), probably his most regularly performed work today. As access to the music of western composers became easier in Eastern Europe, Lutosławski became fascinated by the random element of aleatoric (or chance) music that was being developed in America by composers such as John Cage, and this became a major feature in the dramatic evolution of his own style from 1958. The improvement in East–West relations also brought Lutosławski a major international reputation, leading to many prestigious commissions as well as the honour of being the first-ever recipient of the University of Louisville Grawemeyer Prize (the world's largest and most prestigious composition

Zoltán Kodály (1882–1967)

prize), which he was awarded in 1985 for his Third Symphony (1983).

Similarly, most of Ligeti's output before he was thirty was in a heavily folk-based idiom, with a strong influence of Bartók. As a Jew, he suffered terribly during World War II – he was interned in a Nazi labour camp for two years, and both his father and brother died in Auschwitz. Following the 1956 Hungarian uprising he fled to Austria, where he came into contact with the music of the European avant garde and forged his own personal response to the crisis of modern music: a new style known as micropolyphony. In this, clusters of many overlapping motifs create a cloudlike texture of harmonies which do not change clearly, but rather gradually merge seamlessly into one another. One of the most famous examples of Ligeti's micropolyphonic style is his Requiem of 1965 which was used in Stanley Kubrick's film *2001: A Space Odyssey*. Although this film introduced Ligeti's music to a vast new audience, Kubrick originally used the music without permission, resulting in a long legal battle over breach of copyright. Fortunately, neither party seemed to bear a grudge and Kubrick used Ligeti's piano piece *Musica Ricercata* (1951–3), this time with full permission, in his final film, *Eyes Wide Shut* (1999).

However, the adoption of avant-garde techniques by Eastern European composers did not mean an absolute end to their interest in folk music. Through the complexities and tone clusters of Ligeti's more recent works such as the Viola Sonata (1994), subtle references to the melodic shapes of Romanian folk music can occasionally be found. And the music of Penderecki, who like Lutosławski and Ligeti had embraced a challenging modernist idiom in the 1960s, reverted to a neo-Romantic style in the 1970s, often drawing on folk tradition in works such as the *Polish Requiem* (1984).

Béla Bartók (1881–1945)

Bartók's music stands alone in the history of twentieth-century music. He didn't follow the techniques of any particular compositional school, and although he was certainly influenced by figures such as Richard Strauss, Wagner and Debussy his language was very much his own. Such individuality came at a price, and throughout his lifetime his music was heard far less than it deserved. In his own country he was better known as a virtuoso pianist and an ethnomusicologist than as a composer. Much of Bartók's music is characterised by striking rhythms, often derived from the complex rhythmic nature of Hungarian folk music (mirroring the inflections of the Hungarian language), and by the frequent use of percussive effects, which has led to his music being described as 'primitive'. This is a description of which Bartók himself would have approved. He did not seek to write sentimental music, and whereas other, earlier nationalist composers could be said to have polished the edges of folk music before including its influence in their own work, it was the earthy and often complex nature of traditional music in its original state that Bartók admired and sought to absorb into his own idiom.

Bartók was born in 1881 in the Hungarian town of Nagyszentmiklós (Sînnicolau Mare when it became part of Romania). The seeds of his love of music may lie in his

Béla Bartók (1881–1945)

"For my own part, all my life, in every sphere, always and in every way, I shall have one objective: the good of Hungary and the Hungarian nation."

Bartók, in a letter to his family, 1903

having been kept in isolation for his first five years due to a chronic rash which he developed as a baby: he spent much of this time listening to his mother play the piano. In 1894 he and his now-widowed mother moved to Pozsony (now Bratislava). There he befriended the budding composer Ernő Dohnányi whose encouragement led Bartók to enter the Budapest Academy of Music in 1899 as a piano student.

His passion for folk music began when he overheard Lidi Dósa, a Székely Hungarian woman from Transylvania, singing traditional songs in 1904. He was overwhelmed by the beauty of the music and from this time he set out on many field trips with Zoltán Kodály, recording as much of the music of his native country as he could on an Edison wax cylinder. Over the next thirty years, his research led him beyond the borders of Hungary, to Romania, Bulgaria, North Africa and Turkey. The folk music of these countries also coloured some of his own works, notably the *Romanian Dances* (1915) and the orchestral Dance Suite (1923), the latter written to celebrate the fiftieth anniversary of the union of the cities of Buda and Pest.

The often abrasive quality of Eastern European folk music become an increasing feature of Bartók's own music, with his progressively frequent use of percussive effects. The piano piece *Allegro barbaro* (1911) contains savage rhythms, and the performer is instructed to 'hammer out' dissonant clusters of notes; these elements are developed further in the ballet *The Miraculous Mandarin* (1919), which was banned by the censors due to its depraved plot involving a band of thugs who use a beautiful young girl to lure men into a room so they can rob them. His six string quartets, regarded as among

In the early 1900s, Bartók went on many field trips to isolated Hungarian villages, recording as much traditional folk music as he could. Here, his son Peter recalls his father's stories about these trips:

'At times, when my father and I had dinner alone, he spoke to me of how he searched out isolated villages, most removed from civilization and communication, in order to find the old music of the peasants, unadulterated by outside influences. It was necessary to overcome the people's bashfulness, their mistrust of the man from the city, to make friends with them so as to reduce their inhibitions; to live with them among the most primitive surroundings (no Hilton hotels on the Hungarian plains). My father recalled with amusement the conditions of his travels; it was so hard for me to visualize him, a frail, sensitive man whom I had only known in Western style comfort, to do without proper beds, in houses without bathrooms, and more… Getting to work, to meet the peasants and find those who could sing and were willing to do so, needed contacts; these may have been the local schoolmaster or priest, until some people were found who would sing into the Edison machine's horn. Once inhibition was conquered, word might spread, people might come with suggestions, "so and so knows a lot of songs", etc. Sometime the initial fear of the recording machine might turn into a fascination at hearing one's own voice afterwards, and he found co-operation most of the time. Here, I am certain, my father's personality must have had a soothing quality to overcome the people's initial shyness, just as his manner and approach toward the girls helping in our household brought forth smiles and the elimination of barriers. His attitude was not that of the distinguished professor talking to simple folks. He behaved as a friend. The result was co-operation and respect.'

the greatest since Beethoven, are full of brittle, percussive techniques, such as the idiosyncratic 'snap pizzicato' which requires the players to pluck the strings so hard that they audibly rebound back onto the fingerboard.

As a man who had both experience and a deep appreciation of other cultures, Bartók was horrified by the rise of Fascism in Europe. As Hitler introduced more and more anti-Semitic laws, Bartók banned performances of his music in Germany, despite the fact that the royalties derived from German performances constituted a substantial portion of his income. The slow movement of his String Quartet No. 6 (1939) gives a sense of Bartók's despair at the worsening political situation, and in 1940 he felt he had no option but to leave Hungary, with his wife Ditta, for New York.

Bartók spent the five remaining years of his life in America. This was a far from happy time: his health was poor, he received few performances, and he had little money to support himself. His music underwent a major stylistic shift towards a less brittle and more lyrical language. However, despite his emigration and his adoption of a new musical style, he never forgot his home country. In his Concerto for Orchestra website 16, which he completed in 1943 and which has since become one of the most performed of all twentieth-century works, much of the material of the first movement comes from Eastern European folk music. The violin theme at 3′04″ is based on the rhythm of the *verbunkos*, a traditional Hungarian dance; and the shape and mood of the main theme, heard at 4′03″, is reminiscent of Slovak music.

Bartók died of leukaemia in 1945, just as he was about to complete two new works. A former student, Tibor Serly, put the finishing touches to the Third Piano Concerto and the Viola Concerto. These late works exude a sense of contentment which rarely betray the troubles of Bartók's final years in America, perhaps suggesting that the defeat of the Nazis gave the composer a profound sense of satisfaction and hope for the future of his homeland.

VIII. Music from Behind the Iron Curtain

When the Bolsheviks seized power in Russia in November 1917, they recognised that music, and art as a whole, was a potentially powerful medium which could help them to educate a largely illiterate population in the principles of Marxism. They took control of major artistic institutions such as the Bolshoi and Mariinsky Theatres, and began to vet the repertoire, banning any works that were deemed to stand in opposition to their political agenda. Lenin himself had conservative artistic tastes, so composers with innovative tendencies could not expect to find official favour with the music department of the Ministry of Education. This policy of censorship caused great unease within the artistic community; some composers, Rachmaninov, Stravinsky and Prokofiev among them, decided to emigrate – a move which others scorned, considering it demeaning to their strong sense of Russian national pride.

At the end of the Russian Civil War in 1921 there was a brief period when censorship was relaxed, and during this time works by Schoenberg, Berg and Hindemith received their Russian premieres. But with Lenin's death and Stalin's accession to power in 1924, state control over the arts was once again tightened and the potential consequences for creating 'inappropriate' art became increasingly ominous. Many writers 'disappeared' during Stalin's reign – a euphemistic way of referring to their deportation and execution. Among them were Shostakovich's brother-in-law the physicist Vsevolod Frederiks (1885–1944), and the composers Ivan Sollertinsky (1902–1944) and Nikolay Zhilyayev (1881–1938).

What the authorities wanted from composers were uplifting symphonies, full of patriotic folk-tunes and revolutionary songs to inspire feelings of loyalty among the masses. Modernist tendencies were denounced as 'bourgeois formalism' (ironically, the Nazis, at the opposite end of the political spectrum, had denounced the same tendencies as 'cultural Bolshevism'). There were plenty of composers who obliged the authorities, but the music of composers such as Vladimir Zakharov (1901–1956) and Vano Muradeli (1908–1970) is now long forgotten. Instead it is composers such as **Dmitry Shostakovich** (1906–1975) and **Sergey Prokofiev** (1891–1953) whom we remember today. Both had returned from exile in the 1930s and took major risks to remain true to their inner convictions in a highly repressive society.

After Stalin's death in 1953, there was a period of around ten years known as the cultural thaw when the State once again loosened its iron grip on creativity; but when Leonid Brezhnev became leader of the Soviet Union in 1964, cultural repression took hold of the country once again. Many artists were put on trial, and some were subjected to psychiatric treatment. It was only in 1985 when Mikhail Gorbachev assumed power that Russian artists finally had the chance to enjoy genuine creative freedom once more.

Sergey Prokofiev (1891–1953)
Prokofiev was the last great Russian composer to spend his entire youth in the days of Imperial rule. He was born in the village of Sontsovka in the Ukraine where his father managed a country estate. He inherited his love of music from his mother, Maria Prokofieva, a talented musician who regularly played the piano in the family home. Prokofiev wrote his first piece at the age of five, and Maria, recognising that her son had a natural gift, organised a meeting with the famous Moscow professor Sergey Taneyev. Taneyev arranged for the young composer Reinhold Glière (1875–1956) to spend the summers of 1902 and 1903 in Sontsovka, teaching the young Prokofiev. However, aware that her son could never get a decent musical education living in a remote village, Maria moved with him to St Petersburg in 1904, leaving her husband behind.

In the same year, Prokofiev – at the age of thirteen – became the youngest-ever student to be admitted into the St Petersburg Conservatoire, and soon became known as an *enfant terrible*. His ambition and boundless self-confidence gained him a reputation for arrogance and his dissonant compositions rarely met with approval from his conservative tutors. His first two piano concertos date from his college years, and although these works received a largely positive public response, they were slated by the critics as a cacophonous muddle. Ironically, Prokofiev achieved his greatest success at the Conservatoire by winning the coveted Rubinstein Prize for best pianist with a performance of his own Piano Concerto No. 1 (1912).

After leaving college in 1914, Prokofiev made a trip to Paris, longing to become part of the revolutionary music

Sergey Prokofiev (1891–1953)

"Music has definitively reached and passed the greatest degree of dissonance and of complexity that it is practicable for it to attain."

Prokofiev, quoted in an interview with the critic Olin Downes in *The New York Times*, 1930

scene there which was headed by his fellow-countryman Stravinsky. He became acquainted with Diaghilev who commissioned him to write a ballet, but the score was rejected, presumably because Diaghilev was anxious to avoid a repeat of the riotous scenes encountered at the premiere of *The Rite of Spring*. Prokofiev later reworked the ballet into an orchestral suite which he named *The Scythian Suite*: its harsh, rhythmic idiom duly caused a riot at its premiere in 1916.

In 1917, Prokofiev took refuge in the Caucasus to escape the war-torn streets of Petrograd (as St Petersburg had been renamed in 1914). There he continued to compose prolifically, producing his first real masterpieces, including the First Violin Concerto and the Symphony No. 1 'Classical'. However, the artistic repression introduced by the Bolsheviks, coupled with the general civil unrest, prompted Prokofiev to move to the West in 1918. He spent two years in America where the disillusionment of consistently bad reviews was somewhat alleviated by his meeting Lina Llubera, who was to become his wife, and by receiving a commission from the Chicago Opera for *The Love for Three Oranges*, which became a huge international success. In 1920 he returned to Paris, which he used as his base for the next sixteen years. A successful tour of the Soviet Union in 1927 contributed to a growing sense of homesickness for Russia. From 1933 Prokofiev began to spend more and more time in Moscow, eventually returning there with his family in 1936.

During the 1920s Prokofiev's style had become increasingly complex, but by the early 1930s he had reverted to a more post-Romantic and lyrical idiom. This was just as well, given that his return to Russia coincided with an increased rigour in Stalin's control over the arts. It was around this time that Prokofiev became interested in writing scores for theatre and films; he produced his first film score in 1934 for *Lieutenant Kijé* website 17, directed by Aleksandr Faintsimmer. He created an orchestral suite from the score, and fans of pop music from the 1980s may recognise the main tune of the Romance – Sting used it as a basis for his song *Russians*. This accessible phase of Prokofiev's career also produced the delightful *Peter and the Wolf* (1936), written with the aim of introducing children to the instruments of the orchestra.

The war years saw the composition of some of Prokofiev's finest works, including the ballet *Cinderella* (1944), the opera *War and Peace* (1942) and the Symphony No. 5 (1944). Prokofiev was on a creative high, but this was a turbulent decade for the composer. He left his wife in 1941 to be with the poet Mira Mendelson, whom he had met when working on his opera *The Duenna* (1940) and whom he later married. And his success did not make him immune from brutal censorship by the Soviet government. In 1948 he was devastated when his music – along with that of Shostakovich and several other composers – was denounced by Andrey Zhdanov, a member of Stalin's elite, as too cosmopolitan and formalist. Demoralised and frightened by this experience, he set about writing a number of patriotic but wholly unremarkable choral works in an effort to appease the regime. However, in spite of deteriorating health, Prokofiev showed in later works such as his Symphony-Concerto and the elusive Symphony No. 7, both from 1952, that his true creative genius remained undiminished. Prokofiev suffered a brain haemorrhage on 5 March 1953 and died on the same day, just hours before Stalin.

Dmitry Shostakovich (1906–1975)

Unlike Prokofiev, Shostakovich's formative years were spent after the Russian revolution, and by the time he reached maturity he sympathised with many of the principles of the new Communist regime. Yet even though he had a desire as a composer to serve the state, the government's constantly changing goalposts in terms of what constituted 'acceptable' music made it impossible for him to stay on the right side of the authorities. The fascinating story of his precarious relationship with the Soviet state can be followed through his cycle of fifteen symphonies, which stands out as one of the most important in the history of classical music.

Shostakovich wrote his First Symphony as a graduation piece at the Petrograd Conservatoire in 1925. Its conservative but highly individual style found favour with the government. However, his years at the Conservatoire had come at a time when artistic restrictions had been relaxed, and he had heard much of the exciting modern music that was being written by Western composers. As a result, his own style soon became more complex, and although the modernity of his Second and Third Symphonies, written in 1927 and 1929 respectively, escaped censorship (possibly due in part to their inclusion of choral settings of Marxist texts) it was not long before he had his first run-in with the regime. His opera *Lady Macbeth of the Mtsensk District* (1932) initially enjoyed remarkable critical

The famous Zhdanov Decree of 11 February 1948 began by denouncing the opera *Velikaya Druzhba* ('The Great Friendship') by Vano Muradeli, before embarking on a more general denouncement of the entire Russian musical establishment:

'The main shortcomings of the opera are primarily rooted in its music. The music of the opera is inexpressive and poor.

...The composer has not made use of the wealth of popular melodies, songs, refrains, dance motifs, in which the creative work of the peoples of the U.S.S.R. is so rich and, in particular the creative work of the people inhabiting the Northern Caucuses, in which the action depicted in the opera takes place.

...As far back as 1936, the anti-popular and formalistic distortions in the work of D. Shostakovich were subjected to sharp criticism in the organ of the Central committee of the C.P.S.U. (b), *Pravda,* in connection with the appearance of the composer's opera *Lady Macbeth of Mtsensk...* Then... *Pravda* clearly formulated demands which the Soviet people make of its composers.

Despite these warnings and in the face of the instructions issued by the C.P.S.U. (b)... no reorganisation has been carried out in Soviet music... It is a case of composers adhering to a formalist and anti-popular trend. This trend has found its fullest expression

in the works of composers such as D. Shostakovich, S. Prokofiev, A. Khachaturian, V. Shebalin, G. Popov, N. Myaskovski and others, in whose work formalistic distortions and anti-democratic tendencies in music, alien to the Soviet people and to its artistic tastes, are particularly clearly represented.

...This music is strongly redloent [sic] of the contemporary modernistic, bourgeois music of Europe and America which reflects the marasm [sic] of bourgeois culture, the complete denial of Musical art, the impasse which it has reached.

...In our country, composers are granted unlimited creative opportunities and all the necessary conditions have been established for a true flourishing of musical culture... It would be unpardonable not to make use of all these very rich opportunities and not to direct creative efforts along the correct realistic path.'

Dmitry Shostakovich (1906–1975)

"I always try to make myself as widely understood as possible; and if I don't succeed, I consider it my own fault."

Shostakovich, quoted in Joseph Machlis, *Introduction to Contemporary Music*, 1963

and public success, and received eighty-three performances in Leningrad and ninety-seven in Moscow. However, when Stalin eventually attended a performance, he hated it and stormed out during the final act. Shortly afterwards, on 28 January 1936, *Pravda*, the official Party newspaper, published a venomous attack on the opera, describing it as 'muddle instead of music'. A week later, a further article in the same paper denounced Shostakovich's ballet *Bright Stream* (1935) in a similar manner. Shostakovich knew that such criticism reflected Stalin's personal views and as such could not be taken lightly. He completed his Symphony No. 4 (1934–6) and even put it into rehearsal later in the year; but he had to bow to pressure to withdraw it, and set about finding a way of writing music that would keep the authorities happy while not compromising his integrity as a composer. His Symphony No. 5 (1937) was his peace-offering to Stalin, and following its premiere it acquired the subtitle 'A Soviet artist's response to just criticism'. It was written in a relatively straightforward but powerfully expressive style that would characterise many of his future works. Unhappy at being bullied, however, Shostakovich also began to include in his music secret protests against Stalin's tyranny. His Symphony No. 7 (1941) was ostensibly a patriotic protest against the German siege of Leningrad, though Shostakovich admitted privately that it was equally concerned with the way in which Stalin had destroyed the same city. Later, a personal motif – D-S-C-H (based on the German spelling of his name **D**mitri **SCH**ostakowitsch, 'S' and 'H' being the German letters for the notes E flat and B natural) – was used to emphasise an intense sense of personal tragedy in many of his works, notably the String Quartet No. 8 (1968).

Despite the initial success of Shostakovich's opera *Lady Macbeth of the Mtsensk District,* the official Party newspaper *Pravda* published a damning editorial on 28 January 1936 entitled 'Muddle instead of Music', shortly after Stalin had attended a performance. To contemporary readers, this article may seem like nothing other than a bad review; however, Shostakovich was well aware that such an article could only have been sanctioned by Stalin himself, and that his personal safety would be threatened if he did not change his musical style:

'From the first moment, the listener is shocked by a deliberately dissonant, confused stream of sound. Fragments of melody, embryonic phrases appear – only to disappear again in the din, the grinding, and the screaming... This music is built on the basis of rejecting opera... which carries into the theatre and the music the most negative features of "Meyerholdism" infinitely multiplied. Here we have "leftist" confusion instead of natural, human music... The danger of this trend to Soviet music is clear. Leftist distortion in opera stems from the same source of leftist distortion in painting, poetry, teaching and science. Petty-bourgeois innovations lead to a break with real art, real science, and real literature... All this is coarse, primitive, and vulgar. The music quacks, grunts, and growls, and suffocates itself, in order to express the amatory scenes as naturalistically as possible. And "love" is smeared all over the opera in the most vulgar manner. The merchant's double bed occupies the central position on the stage. On it all "problems" are solved.'

The First Violin Concerto was composed in the year that Andrey Zhdanov issued his violent denunciation of Shostakovich and Prokofiev. Shostakovich's reaction to this was similar to that of his older colleague, in that he was deeply shaken: for the next five years he wrote little beyond film scores and a few patriotic vocal works that posed no risk to his personal safety.

Shostakovich described the day Stalin died – 5 March 1953 – as the happiest day of his life. Finally able to unleash his formerly repressed rage at the dictator, he created a vivid portrait of Stalin's murderous brutality in the second movement of his Tenth Symphony website 18, written the same year. The shrieking woodwind (1′33″–1′44″), the threatening brass (2′31″–2′50″) and the driving rhythm and extensive use of percussion throughout the movement are all typical features of Shostakovich's style. The spring of 1955 saw the composition of a film score for Aleksandr Faintsimmer's film *The Gadfly* (1955), the highly embroidered account of an Italian freedom-fighter's struggle against Austrian domination in the mid-nineteenth century. The film achieved only passing success, but the music has become Shostakovich's best-known such score. Shostakovich's facility as a composer of film music is notable, and even today there are new discoveries being made: for example, the dazzling score for *Odna* (1929–1931), recorded by Naxos in 2007 and reconstructed from the official Russian version of the film. This features a huge orchestra, including a pioneering use of the theremin.

Shostakovich was now largely free to write as he pleased, and only with his Symphony No. 13 'Babi Yar' (1962) – its subject matter including the massacre of over 30,000 Jews by the Nazis over two days in 1941 – did he have another minor brush with the censors due to the Symphony's suggestion of Russian anti-Semitism. After Shostakovich suffered a heart attack in 1969, his thoughts turned to mortality: his penultimate Symphony, No. 14, composed in the same year, is a song cycle set to poems about death. It is one of his most profound and moving works, and he dedicated it to Benjamin Britten with whom he had recently developed a warm friendship. After a second heart attack in 1971 he slowed down considerably and wrote only a few more works before his death in 1976.

IX. The American Tradition

At the beginning of the twentieth century, America was still in the process of establishing its own cultural identity. American musicians were extremely keen to create a distinctive national musical style, but they lacked a home-grown tradition upon which they could build. In an attempt to tackle this problem, in 1891 the founder of the National Conservatory of Music in New York wrote to the Czech composer Antonín Dvořák (1841–1904), inviting him to be its director. Dvořák had created a national musical idiom of international stature for his own country, and the Americans hoped that he could show them how to do the same for theirs. Dvořák spent three years at the Conservatory, between 1892 and 1895, and encouraged his students to draw on the various indigenous and folk traditions in America, pointing specifically towards 'negro melodies and Indian chants' as potential sources of inspiration. Some composers followed his advice, but often the resultant works, such as Arthur Farwell's *Navajo War Dance* (1905) and Henry F.B. Gilbert's *Comedy Overture on Negro Themes* (1906), simply superimposed the borrowed material over an essentially European idiom. In any case, as most

American composers at that time were of white descent, it could be questioned whether it was appropriate for them to forge a national idiom out of traditions which weren't really their own. More significant in the formation of a specifically American idiom were the many popular songs dating from the Civil War years (1861–5), which had become part of the American folk tradition as they subsequently cross-fertilised across the continent. **Charles Ives** (1874–1954) was one of the first composers to make imaginative use of these songs in his own works.

Many of the American composers who played a key role in developing a national musical language studied in Paris with the legendary composition teacher Nadia Boulanger (1887–1979). Boulanger encouraged her American students to regard their lack of a national musical heritage as an advantage: it meant that they didn't need to feel held back by the lofty example of past masters and that they had greater freedom to innovate. During the twentieth century, many of Boulanger's pupils helped America to develop a reputation as one of the most musically progressive countries in the world; they included **Aaron Copland** (1900–1990), **Philip Glass** (b. 1937) and **Elliott Carter** (b. 1908). Carter was initially encouraged to become a composer by Charles Ives, who had sold insurance to his parents. Although Carter's music can't be attributed to any particular school of composition, his consistently innovative and dynamic output of works is unmistakably American. Sometimes it is reminiscent of the vastness of the American landscapes; at other times, his complex counterpoint conjures up the dense and hectic environment of the big cities.

George Gershwin (1898–1937)

Throughout the century, there has generally been much more willingness in America than in Europe to embrace popular genres as 'serious music' – perhaps another advantage of not being chained to the legacy of a long-standing historical tradition. While it was common for European composers to include elements of jazz in their music, this was generally done in a tongue-in-cheek fashion. In contrast, the popular songwriter **George Gershwin** (1898–1937) began in the 1920s to compose fully fledged jazz works for the concert hall, basing them on classical forms. His famous *Rhapsody in Blue* (1924) was an immediate hit with audiences, and Gershwin, keen to demonstrate that this wasn't just a one-off, followed it up a year later with the Piano Concerto in F website 19. The concerto is in a traditional Classical three-movement form: the first movement, making strong use of the Charleston, is followed by a bluesy slow movement, before launching into an electrifying finale. His opera *Porgy and Bess* (1935) went even further in presenting jazz not just as light entertainment but as a type of music that could portray the deepest human emotions.

While music theatre was often regarded as an inferior art form to operas and symphonies, at least in Europe, the conductor and composer **Leonard Bernstein** (1918–1990) was as comfortable writing musicals, such as *On the Town* (1944) and *West Side Story* (1957), as he was his more traditionally classical works, such as the dramatic and beautiful *Chichester Psalms* (1965).

By the 1940s the growth of the film industry was also offering lucrative new opportunities to composers, which must have been a relief given the difficulty of scraping a living by

John Williams (b. 1932)

writing concert music. Many distinguished American composers, including Aaron Copland, **Virgil Thomson** (1896–1989) and **Marc Blitzstein** (1905–1964), combined concert careers with working in Hollywood. (This phenomenon occurred not only in America, but throughout Europe as well – the film activities of other composers such as Shostakovich, Vaughan Williams and Georges Auric have already been mentioned). Nowadays, the world of film is not open to concert composers to the same extent; given the very different skills involved for the screen and for the concert hall, there is a rather unjustly perceived dichotomy between 'commercial' film music and 'artistically pure' concert music. As a result, film and concert composition are regarded as quite different art forms and few composers can successfully bridge this gap. Those who do tend to work in a minimalist style, which is explained in chapter XI.

John Williams (b. 1932) is arguably the greatest and most influential film composer of our era. With around 100 film credits to his name, including *Star Wars, E.T.* and the *Harry Potter* films, he has an unrivalled gift for encapsulating the mood of what is happening on screen. The main theme from his score to Steven Spielberg's *Schindler's List* website 28 captures from its very opening the profound sense of tragedy, suffering and yearning that dominates the film.

Charles Ives (1874–1954)

Today, Charles Ives is regarded as the first great American composer, and indeed one of the most brilliantly innovative musicians of the twentieth century. However, for the majority of his life, his music was rarely performed, and even less often understood by his colleagues. Public acclaim, fortunately, was not at the top of Ives's agenda. He even admitted that he felt freer to experiment and indulge his imagination to the fullest when he knew that there were no plans for his work to be performed. He firmly believed that if his music had any true worth, then it would be discovered in its own good time. And he made a conscious decision not to rely on composition to earn a living: after studying music at Yale, he co-founded a successful insurance agency in New York, leaving composition as a hobby for his spare time.

Ives grew up in Danbury in Connecticut where his father George played an important role in the life of the community – teaching, conducting local bands, and leading the hymn-singing at the outdoor religious gatherings (known as camp meetings). Watching his father hard at work left a deep impression on the young Charles, and many of the imaginative techniques he used in his music can be traced back to his childhood experiences. The majority of his works make use of folksongs (such as *Three Places in New England*, from 1912) and hymns (Symphony No. 3 'The Camp Meeting', written in 1904). His music is often spiky and dissonant, which derives not from the influence of composers such as Bartók and Stravinsky (whose music would have barely been known in America at the turn of the century) but rather from the sound of amateur bands, replete with frequent wrong notes, and players accidentally ending up in the wrong key. The sound of these bands was rough and unrefined, but Ives believed that it was precisely this quality that encapsulated something of the human spirit. He also developed a collage technique by

Charles Ives (1874–1954)

"Beauty in music is too often confused with something that lets the ears lie back in an easy chair."

Ives, quoted in Joseph Machlis, *Introduction to Contemporary Music*, 1963

superimposing different layers of music on top of one another. This might sound complicated but it simply grew out of having heard two military bands simultaneously marching through Danbury playing different pieces. Ives's *Country Band March* (1905) uses collage in a witty but nostalgic evocation of the music he so often heard in his youth. His originality is also demonstrated by his anticipation of Schoenberg's twelve-note row in *Chromâtimelôdtune* (c. 1919), though he didn't subject the row to a Schoenbergian serial treatment.

Many of Ives's pieces were inspired by his great interest in a group of nineteenth-century American transcendentalist philosophers: Ralph Waldo Emerson, Nathaniel Hawthorne, Henry David Thoreau and Bronson Alcott. The most famous of these is *The Unanswered Question* website 21 – from 1906 – which Ives described as a 'cosmic drama'. In the piece Ives makes pioneering use of collage, splitting the orchestra into three groups, and assigning a different aspect of the drama to each group. Underpinning the whole piece, the calm strings evoke 'the silence of the Druids', while a trumpet poses 'the perennial question of existence' a total of seven times. The first six trumpet 'questions' are followed by a group of woodwind instruments – 'the fighting answerers' – who become increasingly frantic and frustrated in their attempt to provide an answer (1′27″, 1′54″, 2′26″, 2′57″, 3′27″, 3′48″). But the trumpet's final question is met with silence, and the piece finishes as it began, with 'the silence of the Druids' and the implication that it is ultimately futile to search for a rational answer to this existential question.

In 1926, Ives suddenly found that his creative powers had left him, and although he continued to revise some of his works, he effectively stopped composing. A few years later, ill-health forced him to take early retirement from the insurance business. It was almost another twenty years before the world began to recognise his achievements and some of his most important works received their first performances. His Symphony No. 3 'The Camp Meeting', from 1904, was finally premiered in 1946, and won the prestigious Pulitzer Prize the following year. Symphony No. 2 (1902) had to wait even longer, remaining unperformed until 1951. His Fourth Symphony (1916) only received its premiere in 1965, eleven years after Ives's death from a post-operative stroke.

Aaron Copland (1900–1990)

"Music that is born complex is not inherently better or worse than music that is born simple."

Copland, quoted in Robert Jacobson, *Reverberations,* 1975

The youngest of five children, Aaron Copland was born and bred in Brooklyn, New York. His parents were Russian-Jewish immigrants and the surname 'Copland' is in fact an anglicisation of the Russian name 'Kaplan'. Copland's first composition tutor, Rubin Goldmark, was a man of conservative tastes who did all he could to discourage what he saw as his pupil's unhealthy interest in avant-garde music, such as that of Charles Ives. But this did nothing to dampen Copland's progressive outlook and he went to Paris at the age of twenty-one, where he became Nadia Boulanger's first American student.

Boulanger was in no doubt that Copland had a unique gift. Before he returned to America in 1925 after four years of study, she offered him his first major commission, to write an Organ Symphony (1924) for her to play on her forthcoming debut tour of the States as an organist. Copland later reworked this piece as his First Symphony (1928).

Keen to write music that took its inspiration from American culture, and perhaps also influenced by Les Six who dominated the Parisian music scene during his years there, Copland produced a string of jazz-inspired works, such as *Music for the Theatre* (1924) and the Piano Concerto (1925). His Piano Variations of 1930, however, marked the beginning of a more dissonant and austere stylistic phase. In around 1936 he became concerned that his more cerebral style was alienating a wider public, and he began to write in a more accessible and distinctly American idiom. His music from this period frequently uses folk elements, such as cowboy songs and the hymns of the Shaker religious community; he also travelled to Mexico several times and wrote a number of works with a Latin flavour, including *El salón Mexico* (1936). It was this phase of his career which yielded Copland's most famous works: *Fanfare for the Common Man* (1942) and the three ballets *Billy the Kid* (1938), *Rodeo* (1942) and *Appalachian Spring* (1944), all of which have since become American classics. His interest in writing music that was popular also resulted in several film scores, including Lewis Milestone's adaptations of John Steinbeck's novels *Of Mice and Men* (1939) and *The Red Pony* (1949).

In 1950, his style changed yet again and, just as Stravinsky had done around the same time, he embarked upon a final creative phase that was based on Schoenberg's serial technique. By this stage his compositional voice was firmly established, and his twelve-note works, such as *Piano Fantasy* (1957) and his last important orchestral work *Inscape* (1967), retain the breadth and expansiveness reminiscent of wide, open American landscapes, which characterised his music.

The early symptoms of Alzheimer's disease became evident in the early 1970s, though for the next decade he continued to compose a little, and also to conduct. He died on 2 December 1990 in North Tarrytown (now Sleepy Hollow) in New York State.

Samuel Barber (1910–1981)

"Most composers bore me, because most composers are boring."

Barber, quoted in David Ewen, *American Composers*, 1982

Although Samuel Barber wasn't part of the American nationalist school of composers, many of his works have become such staples of concert repertoire that they have played a major role in stamping America's mark on the musical map of the world. In contrast to Ives and Copland, Barber wasn't an innovator and his style was conservative; his music has often been referred to as neo-Romantic, hardly a term of endearment in the years of the post-World War II avant garde. But Barber's unrivalled gift for lyricism and fluency meant that his music was always filled with ravishing tunes that seem to outweigh any need or desire for modern techniques.

Born in West Chester, Pennsylvania, Barber entered the Curtis Institute at the age of thirteen to study voice, piano and composition. He had a fine baritone voice and for some years he seriously considered becoming a professional singer, but by the early 1930s he had set his sights on composing. Shortly after graduating, he was awarded the Prix de Rome, and in 1935 and 1936 he received Pulitzer Fellowships which enabled him to develop his career further in Europe. His works from this early period demonstrate his talent for melody, and some – *Dover Beach* and *The School for Scandal* overture, for instance, both dating from 1931 – are still regulars in the concert hall. In 1938 he wrote his *Adagio for Strings*, an adaptation of the slow movement of his String Quartet No. 1, written two years earlier. Around this time, Barber met Arturo Toscanini in Italy; the conductor was so impressed with the *Adagio* that he regularly programmed it with orchestras throughout Europe and America, thus giving the young composer an international platform. Barber's *Adagio* has become one of the best-known pieces of all twentieth-century music, and its poignant use in major films such as David Lynch's *The Elephant Man* (1980) and Oliver Stone's *Platoon* (1986) has brought it to a much wider audience than the classical norm.

Another of Barber's most regularly performed works is the Violin Concerto, written in 1939. This work heralded a new and more progressive phase in Barber's career. The first two movements of the concerto are in typically lyrical style, but the third enters the realms of dissonance and rhythmic complexity. Throughout the 1940s he experimented with different techniques, such as neoclassicism in the *Capricorn*

Concerto (1940) and polytonality (music that is simultaneously in several different keys) in *Essay for Orchestra* No. 2 (1942). He didn't settle on any one particular new style, however, and his natural tendency for pure and unadulterated lyricism, such as in the exquisite *Knoxville: Summer of 1915* (1947), was never far away.

Given his melodic gift, and his training as a singer, it is no surprise that Barber was drawn to the operatic genre. The librettos for his first two operas – *Vanessa* (1957) and *A Hand of Bridge* (1959) – were written by his fellow composer and lifelong partner Gian Carlo Menotti (1911–2007). Both works achieved considerable success, and the former – a dark, Bergmanesque story in which the heroine and her niece vie for the love of her dead husband's son – was awarded the Pulitzer Prize in 1958. But Barber's third opera, *Anthony and Cleopatra* (1966), with a rather overwritten libretto by Franco Zeffirelli, flopped when it premiered at New York's Metropolitan Opera. The terrible reviews of the opera seriously damaged Barber's reputation: organisations lost interest in commissioning him and he lost much of his self-confidence. Although he was never a particularly prolific composer, his creative output in the 1970s slowed significantly after this experience. Right up until the time of his death from cancer in 1981, the preferred aesthetic in the world of new music was geared towards the avant garde and modernist innovation, and Barber's music was deemed too old-fashioned to be worthy of much attention. However, recent years have seen an increased enthusiasm for lush orchestral sounds and today Barber's music is once again receiving the recognition it deserves.

X. The Avant Garde

After the end of World War II came further innovations which began to push music beyond the bounds of what had previously been thought possible. Much of this revolutionary musical activity was focused on the German town of Darmstadt, where a summer school for new music was set up in 1946. Its aim was to promote the progressive musical creativity which had been stifled for so many years by the Nazis. The school quickly developed a reputation as the international centre of the musical avant garde, and talented young composers from all around the world flocked to attend its courses. The avant-garde movement generated feverish excitement, in particular for Eastern European composers who, freed from the shackles of Soviet artistic censorship, fully embraced the chance to explore brand new ideas and techniques. Darmstadt's most illustrious period was in the mid-1950s when courses were led by **Pierre Boulez** (b. 1925), **Karlheinz Stockhausen** (1928–2007) and **Luigi Nono** (1924–1990), who for a few years worked together to explore the possibilities of a new technique called total serialism. Based on an idea introduced by **Olivier Messiaen** (1908–1992) in his 1949 piano piece *Modes de valeurs et* *d'intensité,* this extended the principles of Schoenbergian serialism to aspects of music other than just pitch. In other words, as well as having a row of twelve notes, there were additional rows for rhythm, dynamics (loudness and softness) and articulation (whether a note is to be played smoothly or spikily), all of which would be subjected to serial treatment. The result was a type of music that was extremely highly organised. Although the lack of perceived emotional content of such pieces limited their impact upon audiences, total serialism challenged the basis of the inherited Western music tradition and allowed composers to think of music in entirely new ways.

Electronics also became an extremely important component of the avant-garde contemporary music scene in the 1950s. Musicians had been interested in using electronic technology since the 1920s and several new instruments had been invented which made use of it, among them the ondes martenot (featured most famously in Messiaen's *Turangalîla-symphonie* of 1948), the theremin, and the Hammond organ. The development of the tape recorder in the mid-1940s opened up a vast array of new possibilities, and electronic music studios were established in state-run radio stations and universities throughout Europe and America specifically for composers to write pieces in this exciting new genre.

There are two types of electronic music. The term 'electronic music' itself is used to refer to music created out of sounds that have been manufactured purely by electronic means; Stockhausen's *Studie I* and *Studie II* (1953 and 1954) are the earliest examples of this genre. However, this type of electronic music was pre-dated by *musique concrète,* developed in the late 1940s by the Parisian broadcaster Pierre Schaeffer (1910–1995) and consisting of taped live sounds of any type (e.g. a voice, a car, laughter or even footsteps) which were electronically manipulated and combined in a form of collage. *Symphonie pour un homme seul* (1950) by Schaeffer and **Pierre Henry** (b. 1927) is one of the first instances of *musique concrète*.

In the 1950s, some composers also started to introduce elements of chance into their works, creating what is known as aleatoric music, music of chance, or indeterminacy. The chance element could take place at the time of composition, as in John Cage's *Music of Changes* (1951), for which Cage chose the notes and rhythms by tossing coins (a technique which was based on the ancient Chinese system of wisdom, the *I Ching*). Alternatively, the indeterminacy could involve leaving certain decisions to the discretion of the musicians at the time of performance, as in the case of Stockhausen's *Klavierstück XI* (1956), which consists of nineteen musical fragments, the order, speed and dynamics of which are to be chosen by the pianist.

Many people today find it difficult to regard the avant-garde works of the 1950s and 1960s as 'real' music. But it is important to see them in the context of the time: this was a period when it seemed that the Western classical music tradition had run its course, and avant-garde composers sought to address this dilemma by broadening the definition of what music was, and to conceive it in new ways. By introducing brand new methods of composition and performance, such as sounds taped from nature, and chance inspired by Eastern philosophies such as the *I Ching*, they aimed to break away from the notion that music could only consist of a series of fixed notes on a page, and to explore the possibility that any form of sound – and even silence – could be thought of as music with the potential to enrich our human experience.

These experiments in indeterminacy, electronics, total serialism and other compositional processes caused a massive wave of innovative creativity all over the world. **Iannis Xenakis** (1922–2001) was an important figure in the development of electronic music, and also developed a complex system of composition based on mathematical probabilities. Italian composer **Luciano Berio** (1925–2003) – another member of the Darmstadt inner circle in the mid-1950s – embraced complexity and indeterminacy within an expressive and often theatrical style, drawing on influences ranging from Monteverdi through Mahler to modern jazz.

Together with fellow composer **Bruno Maderna** (1920–1973) Berio co-founded the Studio di Fonologia in Milan, an electronic music studio based at Italian Radio. Throughout his career he had a particular fascination for the human voice, largely inspired by his relationship with his first wife, the American soprano Cathy Berberian. Berio wrote many works specifically for Berberian, exploiting the versatility and theatricality of her voice, such as *Sequenza III* (1966) – a surreal canvas of sung, spoken and garbled phonetic fragments. This was one of a series of seventeen pieces entitled *Sequenza*, each one a virtuoso and experimental musical tableau for a solo performer. Berio's *Sinfonia* (1968) is the most famous example of a particular style that was popular in the 1960s in which composers would write a work based on a pre-

Luciano Berio (1925–2003)

Edgard Varèse (1883–1965)

existing piece of music. The third movement of the *Sinfonia* is a complex and astonishing collage of both musical and literary quotations from Mahler (chiefly from his Second Symphony), Ravel, Debussy and the Irish writer Samuel Beckett.

A further key figure in the avant-garde movement was the French/American composer **Edgard Varèse** (1883–1965) who had been passionate about searching for a new type of music since the early part of the century. After a productive early career, he stopped composing for sixteen years until the explorations into electronic music of his avant-garde colleagues in the early 1950s caused him to take up his pen with renewed vigour. His *Déserts* website 22-23, completed in 1954, juxtaposes live orchestral music with *musique concrète*. The 'déserts' that the composer is depicting are the deserts of the mind: the fear, terror and agony that have been inflicted on man both by the forces of nature and by other men. The third of four orchestral sections embodies a sense of hope (track 22, from 1′00″) from within the darkness, but the final electronic section that follows it (track 23), consisting of manipulated urban sounds, is unrelentingly ominous and terrifying.

Olivier Messiaen (1908–1992)

Messiaen stands out as the only major composer of his generation whose works were inspired by a devout religious faith. From an early age he felt a strong connection with the Roman Catholic Church and this manifested itself in almost every piece he wrote. However, his spiritual interests were wide-ranging, and when he entered the Paris Conservatoire in 1919 he set about studying the scales and rhythms of

Olivier Messiaen (1908–1992)

"Among the artistic hierarchy, the birds are probably the greatest musicians to inhabit our planet."

Messiaen, quoted in Russell Sherlaw Johnson, *Messiaen*, 1975

Hindu, and other Eastern, music. These, as well as a deep reverence for nature, proved extremely important influences on his own music.

In 1931 he was appointed organist of the church of La Sainte-Trinité in Paris, a position which he held for the rest of his life. He composed many organ works throughout his career, and their titles, which include *Apparition de l'église éternelle* ('Apparition of the Eternal Church', 1932), *La Nativité du Seigneur* ('The Nativity of the Lord', 1935) and *Messe de la Pentecôte* ('Easter Mass', 1950), illustrate his profound faith. Messiaen's motivation was clearly to convey a spiritual message through his music, so it is hardly surprising that he disapproved of the generally ironic nature of the neoclassical music which was so fashionable in Paris at that time. He, together with fellow composers **André Jolivet** (1905–1974), **Jean-Yves Daniel-Lesur** (1908–2002) and **Yves Baudrier** (1906–1988), founded a group called La Jeune France to try to instil some gravitas into contemporary French music. However, the start of World War II halted their activities before they had managed to achieve anything.

Messiaen served as a medical auxiliary at the start of the war, but in June 1940 he was captured by the Germans and spent nine months in a prison camp in Poland. The conditions at the camp were appalling, but his faith helped him to survive and inspired him to write *Quatuor pour le fin du temps* ('Quartet for the End of Time', 1941) website 24, its instrumentation governed by the musicians available among his fellow prisoners. The quartet was premiered in the camp in January 1941, in front of thousands of prisoners, with a dilapidated piano and a cello with only three strings. In this work Messiaen used birdsong for the first time. From the outset of the opening movement, which is entitled 'Liturgie de cristal', the clarinet and violin represent respectively the blackbird and the nightingale celebrating the arrival of dawn. To Messiaen, enclosed in a prison camp, the freedom of the birds must have proved an overwhelming source of inspiration, and birdsong – and more generally his wonder in nature – came to feature strongly in his later works.

After his release from the prison camp in 1941, Messiaen returned to Paris, where he was appointed Professor of Composition at the Conservatoire. His pupils included Boulez, Stockhausen and an extremely gifted pianist by the name of Yvonne Loriod. She was the inspiration behind many of Messiaen's subsequent piano works, including *Visions de l'Amen* ('Visions of the Amen', 1943) and *Vingt Regards sur l'enfant Jésus* ('Twenty Gazes on the Christ-child', 1944); and in 1959 she became his second wife (his first wife, Claire Delbos, had died after a long illness). The *Turangalîla-symphonie* (1948) was also in part a declaration of his love for Loriod, and it drew on a multitude of inspirational sources, including the sound of the Javanese gamelan orchestra, exotic Eastern scales, and the vast landscapes Messiaen had seen on an earlier trip to the USA.

Although his influence on Boulez and Stockhausen has led him to be regarded as the 'father of the avant garde', Messiaen believed that a dogmatic adherence to total serialism lacked a sense of wonder at the mystery of life, and instead he looked increasingly to nature for inspiration. His massive work for solo piano, *Catalogue d'oiseaux* ('Bird Catalogue', 1958), was one of the many products of his extensive field research into birdsong (also making significant use of the rhythms of both Hindu and Greek music); and a later work *Des Canyons aux étoiles* ('From the Canyons to the Stars', 1974), written for the 200th anniversary of the Declaration of Independence, is another evocation of the awe-inspiring landscapes of America, and earned him the unusual honour of having a mountain named after him in Zion National Park in Utah. However, his Roman Catholic faith remained the driving force behind his composition, and one of his last achievements was the massive four-hour opera *Saint François d'Assise* which he worked on for eight years, between 1975 and 1983.

Pierre Boulez (b. 1925)

Pierre Boulez is one of the most important musicians of the second half of the twentieth century. Aside from his radical approach to composition, he has held conducting positions with some of the greatest orchestras in the world, and as a theorist he has exerted an influence that few composers over the last fifty years have escaped.

Given his highly ordered methods of composition, it is no surprise to learn that he initially studied mathematics in Lyon, before entering the Paris Conservatoire as a pupil of Messiaen. In the 1940s he began to develop a reputation as a musical revolutionary with a series of works, notably his first two piano sonatas, which set out to rip themselves free from any traditions of the past. As mentioned earlier, it was Messiaen's *Modes de valeurs et d'intensité* which set him on the road to developing the principles of total serialism, of

Pierre Boulez (b. 1925)

"Revolutions are celebrated when they are no longer dangerous."

Boulez, comment made in 1989, from
The Columbia World of Quotations, 1996

which the most famous example is Boulez's fearsomely complex and highly structured song cycle *Le Marteau sans maître* ('The Hammer without a Master', 1954) – a work so technically demanding that fifty rehearsals were needed prior to its premiere. But his period of total serialism lasted only a few years, and from the mid-1950s Boulez began to experiment with other new techniques of the avant-garde scene: *Poésie pour pouvoir* (1958) is scored for three orchestras and electronic tape; and in *Figures, Doubles, Prismes* (1957) and the Third Piano Sonata website 25 he employed indeterminacy. He began writing this Sonata in 1958, and to date it remains officially unfinished. He has written five *formants,* or movements, of which he has so far only allowed two – *Trope* and *Constellation-Miroir* – to be published. The indeterminacy lies in the instruction to the performer to make his or her own choice about the order in which the movements are played. *Trope* is subdivided into four sections – *Texte, Parenthèse, Glose* and *Commentaire* – and again, the performer is free to choose the order of these sections. *Constellation-Miroir* consists of phrases which are followed by arrows pointing to four alternative subsequent phrases, so the way in which the movement progresses is once more determined by the pianist.

Boulez's failure to complete the Third Piano Sonata was symptomatic of a general tailing-off of his compositional activities. As the 1960s progressed he began to dedicate more time to conducting and other projects. In 1970 President Georges Pompidou asked him to set up and direct a new music research institute. This resulted in the foundation of IRCAM (L'Institut de Recherche et Coordination

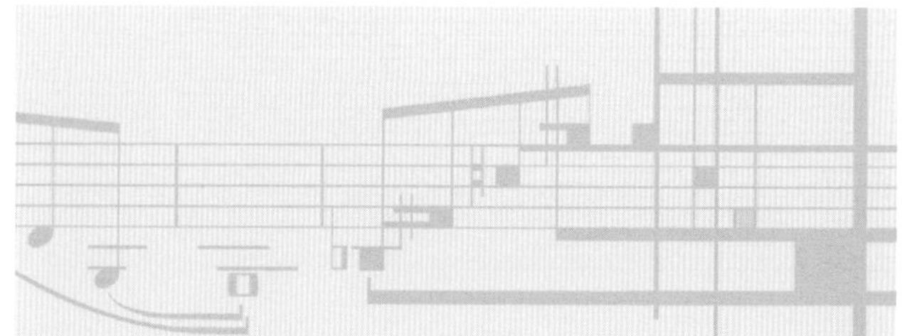

Boulez's music is essentially about control, and Cage's about freedom. However, despite their differing aesthetics they had a deep admiration for each other's work and enjoyed a lively exchange of ideas. In the following extract from a letter dated December 1951, Boulez responds to Cage's description of his use of the *I Ching* in *Music of Changes* which he was in the process of writing:

'The only thing, forgive me, which I am not happy with, is the method of absolute chance (*by tossing the coins*). On the contrary, I believe that chance must be extremely controlled: by using tables in general, or series of tables, I believe that it would be possible to direct the phenomenon of the automatism of chance, whether written down or not, which I mistrust as a facility that is not absolutely necessary. For after all, in the interpolations and interferences of different series (when one of them passes from durations to pitches, at the same moment as another passes from intensities to attacks, etc...), there is already quite enough of the unknown. I am a little afraid of what is called "automatic writing", for most of the time it is chiefly a lack of control. The idea that I find most interesting in all that you have explained to me is the opposition between mobility and immobility of the constitutive elements of a table, on the one hand; on the other, the tables of varying tempi which themselves define the durations... I wait with great impatience for this "Music of Changes", if you cannot send all of it, at least some parts. Especially since it could be played here by Yvonne Loriod.

Acoustique/Musique) – a high-tech music laboratory, with state-of-the-art electronic and computer equipment, and its own resident ensemble, the Ensemble InterContemporain. Boulez visualised a facility where the worlds of science and art would merge, and developed a centre for research into music technology and for the creation and promotion of high-tech contemporary music. IRCAM opened in 1977 in the Pompidou Centre in Paris and was one of the largest, most expensive and most successful musical initiatives in history. To this day, IRCAM remains the international centre of music technology and many important composers regularly use its studios. *Répons*, which was premiered in 1981, is the only major work that Boulez himself has written using the facilities at IRCAM, and we must conclude that, as a composer, he expressed almost everything that he felt he needed to before 1970.

Karlheinz Stockhausen (1928–2007)

When asked once if he had conducted any Stockhausen, the great conductor Sir Thomas Beecham replied, 'No, but I've trodden in some'. Stockhausen's challenging music is certainly not geared towards the conservative ear, but there is no denying that his was one of the most brilliantly inventive and imaginative musical minds of the twentieth century. His development of electronic and computer music influenced as diverse a range of artists as Frank Zappa, Miles Davis, the German arthouse electronic rock group Kraftwerk, Björk, and The Beatles (he even appears on the cover of *Sgt Pepper's Lonely Hearts Club Band*).

Karlheinz Stockhausen (1928–2007)

"Musical form is life-form, thought-form, made audible."

Stockhausen, quoted in Karl Heinrich Wörner, *Stockhausen: Life and Work*, 1973

Stockhausen's childhood was tough. Born in Modrath, near Cologne, he was an orphan by the time he'd reached thirteen: his mother, hospitalised for serious depression in 1932, was put to death under the Nazis' euthanasia programme, and his father was killed in action during the war. After the end of the war, Stockhausen was penniless but paid his way through music college by playing the piano in cafés and restaurants. He subsequently went to Paris to study with Messiaen, and in the first half of the 1950s his career moved in a similar direction to that of his friend Pierre Boulez: he attended courses and later taught at Darmstadt, and he experimented with total serialism in several works including *Kreuzspiel* (1951), *Kontra-Punkte* (1953) and Piano Pieces I–IV (1953). However, Stockhausen showed an earlier interest in electronic music than his colleague did. While in Paris, he spent time experimenting in Schaeffer's *musique concrète* studio, and back in Germany he got a job at West German Radio's newly established electronic studio in Cologne. His objective was to try to produce music created entirely from electronic sources, and it was there that he produced his *Studie I* and *Studie II* in 1953 and 1954. These are based on what are now fairly rudimentary electronic techniques, such as sine waves and the filtering down of white noise into coloured noise.

As technology advanced, Stockhausen led the way in exploring more adventurous forms of electronic music. With the advent of two-track (stereo) output, and then four-track, Stockhausen became fascinated by the effects he could create through having different sounds coming from different directions: in the beautiful *Gesang der Jünglinge* ('Song of the Youths', 1956) five groups of loudspeakers placed around the performance space project a mixture of purely electronic sounds and the electronically manipulated recording of a boy singing. It was the first work to combine *musique concrète* with electronic sounds and marked a milestone in electronic music.

Throughout the 1960s, as Boulez was slowing the rate of his composition, Stockhausen continued to try out new techniques and new technology. He began to use indeterminacy, giving only general guidelines to performers as to the pitch, duration and dynamic of the notes. In works such as *Mixtur* (1964) and *Mikrophonie I & II* (1965) he employed 'live electronics': rather than simply playing a pre-recorded tape, a technician was required to operate electronic equipment, such as ring modulators and sine wave generators, during the performance.

Stockhausen's trip to Japan in 1966 sparked off an intense interest in other cultures: works such as *Telemusik* (1966) – an electronic fusion of religious and folk music from Europe, Asia, Africa and South America – and *Hymnen* (1967), in which forty of the world's national anthems are ingeniously intertwined, are early examples of the phenomenon now known as world music. The seventy-minute *Stimmung* ('Tuning') website 26-29, written in 1968 for six solo singers, is another work which illustrates Stockhausen's fascination with foreign traditions: the text consists of the names of gods and goddesses from many different cultures, as well as erotic poetry written by the composer for his second wife, Mary Bauermeister. The work is remarkable in that it is built entirely out of the harmonics of one bass note (harmonics are 'additional' pitches that occur naturally as part of any note), and in essence the whole seventy minutes consists of just one chord. The effect is mesmerising due to Stockhausen's ingenious textural variation and use of experimental vocal techniques. In the first four sections of the work you can hear some of these techniques, such as the singer gradually changing lip position to colour the timbre of the note (track 26, 0′58″–1′04″), pitched breath (track 26, 1′32″–1′37″), a strange type of nasal chanting (beginning of track 27) and emphatically rolled Rs (track 27, 1′20″–1′30″). In this extract the names of the deities that are incanted are Gott (the German word for God; track 27, 0′43″), Grogoragally (an Australian aboriginal sun god; track 27, 1′13″), the Hindu god Vishnu (track 28, 0′17″) and Elyon (a Hebrew god of storms; track 28, 0′30″).

From 1977 Stockhausen devoted all his compositional energies to one mammoth project of Wagnerian proportions. *Licht* ('Light') is a cycle of seven operas – each named after a day of the week – and represents a consolidation of his musical, religious and cosmological beliefs. In it, Stockhausen continued his quest to extend the possibilities of performance; in 'Helicopter String Quartet' (1993), a scene from *Wednesday*, the performance takes place in the sky, in four helicopters (one for each player), and is projected down to the audience seated in an audio-visual hall. Five of the seven operas – *Monday, Tuesday, Thursday, Friday* and *Saturday* – were premiered between 1981 and 1996; the scenes from *Wednesday* and *Sunday* have been performed individually in concert, but the final two operas in this extraordinary multimedia undertaking have yet to be staged in their entirety.

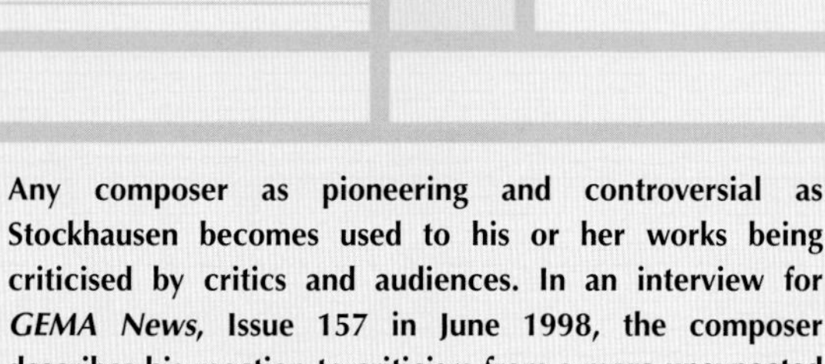

Any composer as pioneering and controversial as Stockhausen becomes used to his or her works being criticised by critics and audiences. In an interview for *GEMA News,* Issue 157 in June 1998, the composer describes his reaction to criticism from a more unexpected source:

'It is a typical reproach that composers of Kunstmusik apparently pollute the environment. It was used against myself in Salzburg during the festival when we were planning to perform the *Helicopter String Quartet.* The Greens in Austria started a press campaign in which they claimed that the environment would be polluted if four helicopters were to fly above Salzburg. At the time they said it was enough if this Stockhausen was performed behind closed doors – the best thing would be if he took off with the helicopters and never came back. Basically this was no more than a journalistic point so that the reactionaries could draw attention to themselves. Personally I wouldn't accept everything as so final. These are basically the strategic steps required to represent material or ideological interests. I believe in the long term this is not at all important. What is important are the works of art laid bare, works that have demanded so much from the world of music-lovers that they provide material for study, for the senses and for discovery. That is the only important thing.'

John Cage (1912–1992)
On the other side of the Atlantic, the key figure in the musical avant garde in America was John Cage. Far away from Darmstadt and the general European infatuation with advanced mathematical systems, Cage's musical philosophy developed in a different – though no less radical – direction from that of Boulez and Stockhausen. To many he seemed like a joker, with his infectious fits of laughter, his strange interests (he was an expert on mushrooms), and his often seemingly absurdist music that valued simplicity over complexity. But his music was an embodiment of Eastern philosophies (in particular Zen Buddhism) that were central to his deep-rooted beliefs about life and spirituality.

Cage grew up in Los Angeles. In his young adult years, he was unsure as to which path he should follow. He toyed with the idea of going into the ministry before deciding to become a writer. He dropped out of college, however, and spent two years travelling around Europe, painting, writing poetry, and – inspired by a blissful summer in Majorca – composing his first pieces of music.

On returning to California, he went to Schoenberg for lessons. It soon became clear to both men that Cage had no feeling for harmony. Schoenberg warned him that this would prevent him from making any headway as a composer, but his teacher's pronouncement only strengthened Cage's conviction that he could succeed. In the 1930s Cage became fascinated with percussive sounds, and he visited junkyards looking for sheets of metal, tram-car springs, brake drums or anything else which could create new and interesting sounds in his pieces. This obsession with percussion eventually led to

John Cage (1912–1992)

"My music liberates because I give people the chance to change their minds in the way I've changed mine. I don't want to police them."

Cage, quoted in *The Observer*, May 1982

his invention of the 'prepared piano', for which he wrote a large body of mesmerising works. This is simply a piano which has had objects such as nuts, bolts, screws and rubber bands placed between or wrapped around its strings. The results are often reminiscent of non-Western music – the Indonesian gamelan orchestra, or the African mbira (thumb piano), for example. His most important work for prepared piano is the *Sonatas and Interludes* website 58 (1946–8), which constitutes Cage's interpretation of the nine 'permanent emotions' of the Indian tradition written about by Hindu philosopher Ananda Coomaraswamy (1877–1947), one of the founders of the Traditionalist school of philosophy. According to Coomaraswamy, there are four 'light' emotions (heroic, erotic, wondrous, mirthful), four 'dark' emotions (sorrow, anger, fear, odiousness), and tranquillity, and all of these are found in both the East and the West. Accordingly, some of the *Sonatas and Interludes* have a drumlike quality that suggests the East, including the First Interlude; others, such as the final *Sonata XVI*, contain bell-like sounds which are clearly European in their inspiration.

As mentioned earlier (see page 105), Cage made use of the *I Ching* to write *Music of Changes* in 1951. Using chance to determine how a piece was written or performed represented Cage's desire, derived from the principles of Zen Buddhism, to remove his own ego and tastes from his music. He went even further towards this goal in 1952 with his most infamous – and, in his opinion, best – work: *4′33″*. This three-movement piece for any instrument or instruments involves the performer(s) coming on stage and not playing a single note for precisely four minutes and thirty-three seconds. What becomes evident during a 'performance' of this work is that it is about not silence but instead the random sounds of the everyday world. Cage remarked that at the premiere, given by the pianist David Tudor in 1952, the audience's attention became focused on the wind outside, the rain falling on the roof and, in the final movement, people talking and walking out of the hall. These are the sounds of real life, according to Cage's philosophy, that constitute 'real' music and that have the power to fill us with a sense of wonder.

From this time onwards, chance elements occurred in every work that Cage wrote. In the 1960s he attracted both cries of ridicule and a cult-following as his work became even more provocative. His *0′00″* (1962) consisted of a performer chopping up vegetables on stage, juicing them in an electric blender, and drinking the result with a microphone attached to his or her throat. In the 1970s, however, Cage reverted to marginally more traditional techniques in a series of instrumental interludes. These included the epic piano work *Etudes australes* (1975), in which the notes were derived – through consulting the *I Ching* – from a map of the Australian sky. He also wrote many works for the dance company of his partner, the renowned choreographer Merce Cunningham, including *Cartridge Music* (1960) for 'amplified small sounds' and *Five Stone Wind* (1988) for percussion and electronics.

Cage was a prolific composer right up until his death, from a stroke, in 1992. He once said that, unlike other composers, he didn't hear music in his head before he wrote it; for him, the purpose of composing was to hear the music that he hadn't yet discovered. He believed that his role as a composer ended with the asking of questions: the answers came from somewhere else. Embracing this philosophy is the key to understanding Cage's music.

XI. Beyond the Avant Garde

Minimalism

In the 1960s a new style developed in the USA which was based on building entire pieces of music out of tiny amounts of material. In part, this style was influenced by the aesthetics of John Cage: the sparse textures of his prepared piano pieces and the Zen concept of stripping the ego from one's own music were clearly important starting points for the development of minimalism. But at the same time it was a reaction against the direction that the avant garde seemed to be taking: some composers felt that the actual *sound* of music was beginning to take second place to an obsession with complexity, indeterminacy and general experimentation. Minimalism also drew on medieval music, which often consists of short repeated melodic and rhythmic phrases.

The first key figure in the minimalist movement was **La Monte Young** (b. 1935). His works include *X for Henry Flint* (1960), in which an unspecified object is repeatedly struck for 'a very long period of time', and *Death Chant* (1961), in which a two-note phrase is very gradually expanded into five notes as a male chorus sings it over and over again. *In C* (1964) by **Terry Riley** (b. 1935), who studied with Young at the University of California in Berkeley, proved to be the seminal work that established minimalism as a major new movement. It employs indeterminacy and is written for 'any number of melodic instruments'. There are fifty-three melodic phrases which must be played in order, but which the musicians can play as many times as they like and at a speed of their own choosing. However, the resulting sound is of vital importance. The note C is played constantly throughout the piece, and the melodic fragments are constructed so as to avoid ugly-sounding clashes, creating a feeling that the work is, as its title suggests, in the key of C. The players are also instructed to listen carefully to each other, and not to stray too far apart, with the aim that the interlocking rhythms and melodies of the various fragments will create a homogenous and compelling aural effect.

Steve Reich (b. 1936)

This idea of interlocking rhythms was developed further by New York-born Steve Reich, the first composer to bring minimalism to a mainstream audience. In the late 1960s he wrote a number of pieces using what he called the 'phase technique'. The principle behind this was that the same music would be played by two or more musicians (or on tape) at very slightly different speeds. So while the two parts start off together, they gradually become out of sync with each other, and new melodies and rhythms unexpectedly appear from the blend of the interlocking parts until they eventually come back into synchronisation. *Come Out* (1966), *Piano Phase* (1967) and *Violin Phase* (1967) are all

Steve Reich (b. 1936)

"In African music there are what they call 'changing patterns'. Very simple patterns that sort of stick out because they're so simple. That means, 'Get ready, and off we go!'"

Reich, in an interview with Gabrielle Zuckerman,
American Public Media, July 2002

examples of this style. The first movement of the 1985 work *New York Counterpoint* website 31, while not an example of phase music, is a good example of the effect of interlocking textures, and of the pulsating harmonies that are typical of Reich's style. It can be performed either by eleven clarinets, or, as on the recording heard here, by a single player who plays one part against a tape of all the other parts which he has recorded separately – a process known as multi-tracking. In the section beginning at 1′30″, you can hear how the various phrases played by the clarinet on different tracks blend together, new melodies and rhythms emerging from the combined texture.

Phase music was constructed primarily out of melodies. However, by the mid-1970s Reich's works were displaying a more harmonic basis. *Music for 18 Musicians* (1976) uses rhythms and harmonies which call to mind Indonesian gamelan and West African music, both of which Reich had studied. In the 1980s, Reich began to explore historical and contemporary themes in his work, often drawing on his own Jewish heritage. *Different Trains* (1988) is a poignant work which compares the train journeys that the composer used to make as a child, travelling coast-to-coast, with those that would have likely brought him to his death in a concentration camp had he instead grown up in Nazi-occupied Europe. The piece is written for string quartet and taped voices of Holocaust survivors and a retired Pullman porter.

Reich has also worked with his wife, the video artist Beryl Korot, to produce a number of ambitious multimedia works. *The Cave* (1983) is a two-and-a-half-hour fusion of music and video footage of interviews with Arab and Israeli residents of

Jerusalem expressing their views on Middle Eastern history, all projected onto five screens. *Three Tales,* which was begun in 1998 and premiered in 2002, is another multimedia collaboration between Reich and Korot. It consists of three 'video operas' about major events in twentieth-century history: the crash of the Zeppelin Hindenburg in 1939; the nuclear tests at Bikini Atoll in the South Pacific in the 1950s; and the cloning of Dolly the sheep in 1996.

Philip Glass (b. 1937)

"I think it's more difficult to be a young writer or composer today than it was thirty-five years ago. It's a harsher environment."

Glass, quoted in Robert Maycock, *Glass: A Portrait,* 2002

Philip Glass, the other founder of the minimalist movement, is probably the most commercially successful serious composer working today. He grew up in Baltimore, and after studying with Milhaud in Aspen, and Boulanger in Paris, he got his first job assisting the legendary Indian musician Ravi Shankar on the soundtrack to Conrad Rooks's 1966 film *Chappaqua.* This job was significant for two reasons. First of all, it heralded the beginning of Glass's fascination with non-Western music; this was an important influence on his own music, and it led him to embark on study trips to North Africa and the Himalayas. The job also marked the beginning of his involvement with film music: in addition to his work for the concert hall and the opera house, he is now one of

In the programme note for a concert of his music at New York's Guggenheim Museum in May 1970, Steve Reich made a number of predictions about the future direction of music. Several decades on, we can see that many of these have proved to be correct:

'Electronic music as such will gradually die and be absorbed into the ongoing music of people singing and playing instruments.

Non-Western music in general and African, Indonesian, and Indian music in particular will serve as new structural models for Western musicians. Not as new models of sound. (That's the old exoticism trip.) Those of us who love the sounds will hopefully just go and learn how to play these musics.

Music schools will be resurrected through offering instruction in the practice and theory of all the world's music. Young composers/performers will form all sorts of new ensembles growing out of one or several of the world's musical traditions.
Serious dancers who now perform with pulseless music or with no music at all will be replaced by young musicians and dancers who will reunite rhythmic music and dance as a high art form.

The pulse and the concept of a clear tonal centre will re-emerge as basic sources of new music.'

Hollywood's most sought-after film composers, having written scores for such major productions as *Kundun* (1997), *The Truman Show* (1998) and *The Hours* (2002).

Glass's brand of minimalism resembles Reich's in the way that it is built out of the repetition and gradual transformation of small, pulsating rhythms and melodies. However, he has developed a style, with its distinctive chord progressions, that is instantly recognisable as his own. His early works, such as *Piece in the Shape of a Square* (1967) and *Music in Similar Motion* (1969), tend to be purely abstract in their conception, but from the mid-1970s he began to focus primarily on music for the stage. Glass's major operatic breakthrough came in 1976 with *Einstein on the Beach*, the first of several collaborations with the visionary director Robert Wilson. The success of this opera – an epic and overwhelming meditation on the positive and negative possibilities of Einstein's theory of relativity – did much to reinvigorate the international contemporary opera scene. He followed it up with two further 'portrait operas': *Satyagraha* (1980), based on the life of Gandhi with text taken directly from one of the most important of the Hindu scriptures, the *Bhagavad-Gita*; and *Akhnaten* (1984), based on the life of the Egyptian pharaoh who attempted to establish the first ever monotheistic religion. Glass continues to draw on Eastern traditions in his recent work: *Monsters of Grace* (1997), a multimedia collaboration with Robert Wilson, is based on the poetry and philosophy of the thirteenth-century Persian Sufi mystic Jalaluddin Rumi.

Minimalism in Europe

By the early 1970s, the music of Reich and Glass was becoming well known internationally, and many young European composers began to explore the possibilities of minimalism in their own music. In England, **Michael Nyman** (b. 1944) studied composition at the Royal Academy of Music in London, but in 1964, after becoming disillusioned with the modernist music scene, he stopped composing to embark on a career as an academic, critic and editor. (Nyman in fact was the first person to coin the term 'minimalism' in relation to music, in his 1974 book *Experimental Music: Cage and Beyond.*)

In 1968 a BBC broadcast of Reich's *Come Out* introduced him to a new type of music which convinced him that here was a way forward. Nyman has indeed forged a highly successful career out of a distinctive brand of minimalism, characterised by a powerfully energetic and often harsh orchestral sound, with an equal focus on music for live performance and film scores. In the 1980s he enjoyed a productive collaboration with the director Peter Greenaway, writing scores for films such as *A Zed and Two Noughts* (1985) and *The Cook, the Thief, his Wife and her Lover* (1989). His music for Jane Campion's film *The Piano* (1993) is one of the most popular film scores ever written. Nyman has written more than 200 concert works, most notably the 1986 chamber opera *The Man who Mistook his Wife for a Hat* (a poignant piece based on a book of case studies by neurologist Oliver Sacks), four string quartets, the Trombone Concerto (1995) and the Double Concerto for Saxophone and Cello (1997).

As minimalism became absorbed into the general musical consciousness composers began to blend it with other styles, and their music is often categorised, rather vaguely, as 'post-minimalist'. **Louis Andriessen** (b. 1939), Holland's leading composer, has achieved international renown for works which combine many different influences, including minimalism, Stravinskian rhythmic momentum, and jazz. Similarly, the music of the English composer **Gavin Bryars** (b. 1943) is a fusion of minimalist, classical, jazz and avant-garde techniques. Bryars has also worked with the experimental rock artist Aphex Twin, and collaborations of this type have helped to break down some of the barriers that exist between 'serious' and 'popular' music. The wide appeal of minimalist-based music has caught the imagination of many rock musicians and has led to several other high-profile artistic collaborations: Philip Glass has worked with David Bowie and Brian Eno, and his *Low* and *Heroes* symphonies of 1992 and 1996 are based on the Bowie albums of the same names; Michael Nyman has worked with Blur's Damon Albarn as well as the British rock band The Divine Comedy.

John Adams (b. 1947)

Like Michael Nyman, American composer John Adams went through a period of disillusionment with the contemporary music scene in the 1960s. To him, it seemed like an elitist club which would only admit the composers who were writing highly complex music. Adams was attracted to Cage's Zen-inspired aesthetic, but he felt that even Cage's music was over-intellectualised. So when he first heard the music of Reich and

John Adams (b. 1947)

"People want to be prodded and challenged by art, not merely consoled with the familiar."

Adams, in an interview with Elena Park for www.andante.com, November 2001

Glass, it came as a revelation to him: here was a style of music that had more to do with tonality and popular culture than cerebral concepts.

The first work that brought Adams to international attention was the orchestral *Shaker Loops* (1978), and it was when describing the style of this piece that Adams coined the term 'post-minimalism'. The work depicts Adams's imagining of the religious ceremonies within the Shaker community, which had settled near his childhood home in New Hampshire. Though undeniably based on minimalist principles, it is less concerned with restricting the amount of musical material and contains much greater contrasts of harmony and dynamics than earlier works by Glass and Reich. Over the next few years Adams developed a style which set Romantic-sounding harmonies against a minimalist texture; and in 1985, with a touch of irony, he named a major orchestral work *Harmonielehre,* after Schoenberg's treatise of 1911 which claimed that late-Romantic music had heralded the end of tonality. One of his most frequently performed works is the exhilarating *Short Ride in a Fast Machine* website 32, written in 1986.

Like so many of his minimalist colleagues, Adams has made a significant mark on the operatic scene. For the first two of his five operas to date, he made politically bold choices of subject matter from recent history. *Nixon in China* (1987) is based on President Richard Nixon's historic diplomatic visit to China in 1972 to meet Chairman Mao; and *The Death of Klinghoffer* (1990) is about the 1985 hijacking of a cruise liner by the Palestinian Liberation Front, and the murder of one of the hostages, a disabled Jewish man named Leon Klinghoffer. It is a riveting drama and a serious exploration – seen from both sides – of a subject which was to become one of the darkest and most important issues of global affairs just over a decade after the work's composition.

'Holy minimalism'?

The term 'holy minimalism' was coined – somewhat disparagingly – to describe a handful of composers whose beautifully contemplative and immensely popular music is a direct expression of their deeply held religious beliefs. The three main protagonists of this style are **Henryk Górecki** (b. 1933) from Poland, the Estonian **Arvo Pärt** (b. 1935) and the English composer **John Tavener** (b. 1944). In fact, the term 'minimalism' is rather misleading here: although the sparse textures, frequent use of repetition, and hypnotic quality of their music do have parallels with minimalist music, their styles did not grow out of the tradition founded by Riley, Reich and Glass. Whereas minimalist composition is essentially about subjecting small amounts of musical material to various processes, the fundamental goal of Górecki, Pärt and Tavener has been to remove all systems and processes from their music. To them, music should be a pure and ego-less embodiment of their spiritual beliefs. In that respect, they have something in common with John Cage, though the results are very different.

After exploring neoclassicism, the avant garde, and collage techniques in the 1960s, Pärt developed an idiosyncratic sound based on a technique which he refers to as 'tintinnabuli': it evokes the pealing of bells by the soft

Arvo Pärt (b. 1935)

"I have discovered that it is enough when a single note is beautifully played."

Pärt, quoted in Nick Kimberley *Arvo Pärt: A Portrait,* 2005

John Tavener (b. 1944)

"The only goal that I've really been committed to all my life... is simplicity."

Tavener, in conversation with David McCleery, 2004

repetition of triads (chords of three notes, commonly the root, 3rd and 5th of a scale). The simplicity of his style is based on his belief that a single note, beautifully played, is all that is needed to touch the depths of the soul. The spellbinding effect of such simplicity can be heard in his *Cantus in Memoriam Benjamin Britten* (1976), which consists essentially of a descending minor scale. A substantial portion of his catalogue of around eighty works is vocal. He has written a number of large-scale choral works, such as *Passio* (1982) and the eighty-minute *Kanon Pokajanen* ('Canon of Repentance', 1998), as well as a large number of shorter choral pieces.

Tavener, by far the most prolific of the three, became disillusioned with Western religion, and more generally with the foundations of Western society, in the 1970s, embarking upon a spiritual quest which led him to join the Russian Orthodox Church in 1977. He studied the music of both the Greek and Russian Orthodox Churches in the early 1980s, and their exotic sounds coloured much of his music throughout the 1980s and 1990s. While Tavener was developing this new contemplative style his public profile faded; but he made a dramatic comeback in 1989 with his work for cello and strings *The Protecting Veil*. In addition to many large-scale works, he has written a considerable number of short *a cappella* choral works, including *Song for Athene* (1993), which was performed at the funeral of Diana, Princess of Wales, and his 1999 setting of *The Lord's Prayer* website 55.

Górecki's early works were influenced by Messiaen, with whom he studied briefly in Paris in the early 1960s. However,

Henryk Górecki (b. 1933)

the Communist officials' stark disapproval of his music resulted in his looking towards folk music as a basis for his works, such as *Three Pieces in Olden Style* (1963). His growing interest in religion became evident in his Second Symphony (1972), which sets a text by the astronomer Copernicus in praise of God. However, all Górecki's previous achievements were eclipsed by the success of his Symphony No. 3 'A Symphony of Sorrowful Songs' website 34, written in 1976. It is a setting for soprano and orchestra of two lamenting prayers and a folksong about a mother grieving for her lost son. In the first movement, a fifteenth-century lamentation is flanked by an expansive and serenely beautiful fugue. The text of the second movement is a prayer that was found scratched onto the wall of a Gestapo prison cell by a young Polish woman. In the first section (0'00"–1'04") a short phrase is repeated a number of times, and in the subsequent section a small fragment is repeated and gradually expanded into a melody. Górecki builds the entire third movement on similar principles. Despite the limited number of musical ideas, the music does not sound minimalist in the traditional sense as Górecki does not apply any processes to the material; instead he simply reiterates and gradually adds to it in order to create a mantra-like meditative effect. Over a million CDs of the Third Symphony have been sold, but despite his worldwide fame Górecki has chosen to stay out of the public spotlight as much as possible. He has composed very few works since 1980, preferring to spend a quiet and tranquil life in his home in the Tatra mountains.

Many composers branded with the label of 'holy minimalist' are of the opinion that Western music of the last fifty years has become so intellectualised that it is longer capable of touching the soul of the listener. In an interview with David McCleery in 2003, John Tavener explains his own views:

'Modernism cannot envisage any kind of Source. Modernism isn't something that I've turned my back on totally: I listen to the music of modern composers, I listen to the music of young composers, I listen to the music [on the radio] every Saturday evening when contemporary music is performed between about eleven and two o'clock in the morning, but I've never found as yet anything within modernism that has brought forth God. I've never found anything within it that I'm able to interiorise, and if you cannot interiorise a sound, then clearly the music has no spiritual possibility. One could take one exception. I think of the music of Webern, for instance, as miraculous, and as a true epiphany. He was a mystic, a nature mystic. His early music is wonderful because one has no idea where it comes from. And then the late serial music, the two cantatas, the late Piano Variations – this music can be internalised, because it's so transparent. He's a one off, he's the only one composer amongst the modernists that makes any impression on me, and in fact I don't really think one should regard him as a modernist at all. He was a mystic.'

XI. A Second Musical Renaissance in England

For the first half of the twentieth century, Britain remained largely untouched by the musical innovations that were taking mainland Europe by storm. During this time, British music was largely defined by the pastoral style, and although composers like Britten and Tippett did adopt a more modern idiom, it was a conservative modernism compared with the atonality and broader experimentation happening in mainland Europe and America.

In Manchester in the early 1950s, student composers **Sir Harrison Birtwistle** (b. 1934), **Sir Peter Maxwell Davies** (b. 1934) and **Alexander Goehr** (b. 1932) all shared a burning desire to soak up as much as they could of the radical musical developments in Europe but found that they were hindered by a general lack of progressive musical attitudes in Britain. In 1953 they, together with the conductor Elgar Howarth and pianist John Ogdon, decided to take matters into their own hands: they formed the New Music Manchester Group specifically to give performances of their own music alongside works by avant-garde European composers. Today, with so much information at our fingertips, it is easy to underestimate how pioneering this move was:

Sir Harrison Birtwistle (b. 1934)

"Violence is a by-product of my music, it's not something I put in... it's the nature of the material I use, perhaps, that equates with violence."

Birtwistle, in an interview with Kirk Noreen and Joshua Cody for www.sospeso.com, September 1999

scores of contemporary European works were practically unattainable at this time in Britain, and they were only able to get hold of much of the sheet music through contacts of Alexander Goehr's father, who had studied with Schoenberg.

Maxwell Davies and Birtwistle subsequently went on to form a professional new music ensemble called The Pierrot Players – later renamed The Fires of London – for which they wrote a large number of bold, modernist works, often theatrical in conception; the group took their music on tour around Britain in the 1960s and 1970s. Although the members of the Manchester Group eventually went their separate artistic ways, they did succeed in creating an avant-garde music scene in Britain. The results could be seen in the work of the next generation of composers, born in the 1940s, who strove to broach new styles and to break new musical ground, thereby bringing British composers into line with the cultural aspirations of their European counterparts. Gone were the days of an easily recognisable national musical language; it was now a time of musical pluralism: many different styles and sources of inspiration co-existed and composers could focus on whichever one they liked, be it the complexity of **Brian Ferneyhough** (b. 1943) and **Michael Finnissy** (b. 1946), the post-minimalism of Michael Nyman and Gavin Bryars, or the deeply held spiritual faiths of John Tavener and the Scottish composer **James MacMillan** (b. 1959).

Sir Harrison Birtwistle (b. 1934)

Even in this broad-minded musical age, the music of Sir Harrison Birtwistle remains provocative and controversial, loved by some and hated by others. The raucous music and murderous brutality of the plot of his opera *Punch and Judy* (in which poor Judy gets murdered no fewer than four times) so shocked Benjamin Britten during its premiere at the 1968 Aldeburgh Festival that he refused to come back after the interval; and almost thirty years later, the outraged reaction of the audience to the premiere of his savage saxophone concerto *Panic* (1995) at the Last Night of the Proms in London entered the annals of musical history.

Birtwistle's music is often described as raw, primitive and ritualistic. The powerful energy of the music does indeed seem to surge forth from some elemental source, as in his orchestral masterpiece *Earth Dances* (1986) – a musical depiction of the shifting strata of the earth's crust. His musical idiom is often harsh and brutal. His chamber work *Tragœdia* (1965) – the first work which announced him as a major international talent – is filled with the screeching sound of woodwinds and other violent gestures. It was a precursor for the opera *The Mask of Orpheus* (1973–84), and this, rather than being a fey retelling of the myth of Orpheus and Euridice, mirrored the violence of *Tragœdia* both through its music and its on-stage action, which includes several violent deaths (by hanging, thunderbolt and dismemberment). Drama – and in particular Ancient Greek drama – has been extremely influential in much of Birtwistle's work, in both structure and subject matter. It was central to the conception of *Tragœdia,* in which Birtwistle gave roles to each of the three instruments (the cello and horn as protagonists, and the harp as mediator), thus creating a dramatic scenario that was implied rather than enacted. This 'abstract dramatic' structure was popular with a number of British composers in the 1960s and 1970s.

If Birtwistle's music can be said to have a central source of inspiration, it is the elemental forces of the natural and the human worlds, and while violence is a part of that, so is beauty. Lyricism is a strong feature in many of his works, for instance *The Fields of Sorrow* (1971) and his more recent opera *The Last Supper* (2000). In the extracts from *Gawain's Journey* website 35–36 he juxtaposes lyricism with aggression. The music from this orchestral work is taken from his opera *Gawain* (1991), based on the Arthurian myth of *Sir Gawain and the Green Knight.* The opening section, track 35, is a gentle lullaby, played to Gawain by the Lady of the Castle of Hautdesert who is trying to seduce him. Soothed by the music, Gawain has the first of three 'Visions of the Hunt' (beginning track 36, 0′00″). The bugle-calls from 0′42″ herald the approach of the hunt, which evidently turns bloody around 1′01″.

Sir Peter Maxwell Davies (b. 1934)

"...in those very early years at university occasionally you'd hear or be able to get hold of a score of something like Boulez's Second Piano Sonata, or some of those early Nono things, or Stockhausen's **Kontra-Punkte.** ***Those pieces triggered something off: they were very liberating."***

Maxwell Davies, quoted in Paul Griffiths, *Peter Maxwell Davies*, 1982

In 2004 Sir Peter Maxwell Davies – or Max, as he is affectionately known to music lovers – was appointed to the royal position of Master of the Queen's Music, and it is a tribute to the work of the Manchester Group that a composer who was regarded as an angry young rebel in the 1950s and 1960s has now been accepted into the heart of the British establishment.

After leaving the Royal Manchester College of Music, he embarked on further periods of study in Darmstadt, Rome and Princeton University. When he returned to England in the mid-1960s, he was writing works in a wildly avant-garde style which shocked and disturbed audiences. *Revelation and Fall* (1965) and *Eight Songs for a Mad King* (1969) are two key pieces from this period, both of them theatrical monologues written for The Pierrot Players. The former features a scarlet-clad nun, at times screaming through a loudhailer, and the latter is a dramatic depiction of the insane King George III of England trying to teach his birds to sing. In 1969 Maxwell Davies's *Worldes Blis*, a seminal orchestral work of the time, caused large numbers of people to walk out of the hall during its premiere at the BBC Proms (this outraged reaction was almost a mark of status for any self-respecting modernist composer).

In 1971 Maxwell Davies settled in the remote Orkney Islands off the north coast of Scotland, after which time his music became less radical, though no less imaginative and individual. His works were now composed in more conventional genres (he began his great symphonic cycle in 1978) and the music gained a more recognisably tonal base. He also indulged his love of early music: in 1970 he completed an opera based on the life of the sixteenth-century English composer John Taverner (not to be confused with the modern John Tavener), and he wrote further chamber works based on music by not only Taverner but also Henry Purcell and Carlo Gesualdo (c. 1561–1613).

One of Maxwell Davies's greatest qualities as a musician is his ability to involve himself with both performers and the community at large, and to draw out of them a personal and human connection with his music. In 1977 he founded the St Magnus Festival on the Orkney Islands with the intention that it should benefit as wide a section of the community as possible. Many of his works for the festival have been written for local schoolchildren to perform, and are based on subjects of regional interest. (In this respect he may be thought to have taken over Britten's legacy of creative and pioneering musical education.) Between 1986 and 1996, he worked closely with the Scottish Chamber Orchestra to write ten 'Strathclyde' Concertos, with solo parts written specifically for individual players from the orchestra.

Maxwell Davies has over 200 published works to his name, including eight symphonies, sixteen concertos, five operas and countless works for young performers. After completing his *Antarctica Symphony* in 2000 (which involved a three-week research trip to the world's southernmost continent), he decided to dedicate his energies to chamber music. A recent project was to write a series of ten string quartets, commissioned by Naxos.

XII. Into the Present

'New tonality'

From the 1970s, the radicalism of the avant-garde scene slowly began to wane and many composers began to have doubts that hardcore atonality and complexity represented the way forward for classical music. Certainly, there was a growing feeling that the increasingly technical and intellectualised approach of some composers to their craft was taking precedence over the resulting sound, thereby alienating their audiences. In 1973 Leonard Bernstein was invited to give the prestigious annual series of Norton Lectures at Harvard University. In them he argued that when presented with a section of atonal music, such as one of Schoenberg's note rows, the human ear would instinctively try to find some tonal implications within the notes. Similarly, Steve Reich in his *Writings about Music*, first published in 1975, predicted that tonality would re-emerge as a foundation for new music. To a considerable extent he was right. Reich's own pieces, as well as those by composers such as Glass, Tavener and Pärt, are the most obvious examples of a return to tonality. But other figures who worked in denser and more intricately argued musical structures also began to embrace tonality. As we've seen, this was a feature of Maxwell Davies's stylistic change in the 1970s; many others also moved in a similar direction – Krzysztof Penderecki, for instance, and the important German composer **Hans Werner Henze** (b. 1926). From neoclassical beginnings, Henze's music progressed through the rigours of Darmstadt and an angular, highly politicised phase inspired by a Communist ideal (his Symphony No. 6 is based on revolutionary songs), eventually arriving at a sensuous lyricism which he feels reflects the free and relaxed environment of Italy, where he has lived happily since 1953.

Such a rediscovery of tonality in no way suggests that music has become old-fashioned or harmonically unoriginal; rather, composers have found a way of writing fresh, challenging, and often dissonant music that retains the sense of a home key. And if you listen to music written at the end of the twentieth century and the beginning of the twenty-first – be it the symphonies of the American **John Corigliano** (b. 1938), the orchestral works of the Finn **Kaija Saariaho** (b. 1952) or the operas of the young British composer **Thomas Adès** (b. 1971) – you often discover extraordinarily lush and imaginative sound-worlds that are essentially rooted in tonality.

So, does this mean that the atonal and avant-garde revolutions of the twentieth century were a waste of time? Clearly, the answer to this question is a resounding 'no'. Although serialism, for example, had more or less ceased to be used as a strict technique by the 1980s, its principles profoundly influenced the way in which composers thought. The English composer **Richard Rodney Bennett** (b. 1936) studied with Boulez in the 1950s and says that he is often surprised to look at scores of his recent tonal works and find that he has sometimes subconsciously subjected his melodies to serial treatment. Similarly, the extensive work carried out by Stockhausen and Boulez may not have created a world in which computers have taken over from the symphony orchestra, but for a considerable number of composers today electronics are an essential ingredient. Many different musical techniques were invented in the twentieth century, and even if none of them single-handedly defined how music would be written in the future, they all played an important part in leading us to the culturally vibrant time of today.

Consolidation

So much has changed in a century. At the end of the Romantic era the musical world was largely dominated by just a few countries, with the vast majority of major composers coming from Germany, Austria, Russia and a number of other Eastern European nations. Today, any list of important contemporary composers will include names from all over the world. The twentieth century has shown that it only takes one charismatic figure to kickstart a new and enduring musical tradition. In England, Elgar was the catalyst; and it is thanks to the legacy left by Sibelius and Nielsen that Finland and Denmark are among the most musically prolific countries of today. They are producing some of the most internationally respected composers of our time, such as the Finns Kaija Saariaho and **Magnus Lindberg** (b. 1958), and Danes **Per Nørgård** (b. 1932) and **Poul Ruders** (b. 1949).

It is not just in Europe and America that this has occurred. Far away from the Western world, **Tōru Takemitsu** (1930–1996) introduced a fascinating and productive classical music tradition into Japan, where Western music had been banned during World War II. Influenced by Stravinsky, Messiaen and Cage, as well as by the traditional music of Japan, his work is an authentic fusion of East and West. This can be heard in his 1971 work *Voice* for solo flute website 57, which combines the percussive stylised idiom of traditional Noh drama with experimental avant-garde note-manipulation techniques, such as application of excess breath (0′35″–0′39″ and 2′10″–2′12″) and using harmonics to sound two notes simultaneously (0′56″–1′00″ and 1′40″–1′42″); the player is also instructed to recite through the instrument the French translation of a line of Japanese poetry.

It will be many years before the vast musical developments of the twentieth century can be put into any definitive context. Each innovation must filter through several generations of composers before its true impact on a common musical language can be gauged. Only in recent years have we begun to evaluate the legacy of the experiments and new ideas of the century's first six decades, such as Schoenbergian serialism, and the early avant-garde work of Stockhausen and Boulez. It can be frustrating not to be able to judge categorically which pieces of music being written today will have long-term importance and influence. The huge proliferation of musical styles, genres and techniques in common use today, combined with the impossibility of knowing whether each one will still fascinate audiences in fifty or a hundred years' time, makes some

Tōru Takemitsu (1930–1996)

people wonder if we have lost our way, or even if the Western classical music tradition has finally run its natural course. But it would be wrong to let ourselves be defeated by the current bewildering abundance of musical creativity. The very fact that we live in a time of unprecedented cultural diversity can only be a positive thing. We may not understand it all yet; we may not be able to see where it is all leading. But perhaps it is not for us to try to answer all these questions. For so long as creative talent has an outlet, music – as it always has done – will find its own future.

Sources of Featured Panels

Page 17: Lesure, François and Nichols, Roger, eds, *Debussy Letters*, Faber and Faber Ltd, 1987

Page 47: Boucourechliev, André, trans. Martin Cooper, *Stravinsky*, Victor Gollancz Ltd, 1987

Page 58: Mitchell, Donald and Reed, Philip, eds, *Letters from a Life*, Vol. 2, 1939–45, Faber & Faber, 1998

Page 72: Bartók, Peter, *My Father*, Bartók Records, 2002

Pages 82–3: Zhdanov Decree, extracts, from *DSCH Journal* No. 9, summer 1998, www.dschjournal.com

Page 86: Gutman, David, *Prokofiev*, Omnibus Press, 1990

Page 116: Nattiez, Jean-Jacques, ed., *The Boulez–Cage Correspondence*, Cambridge University Press, 1990

Page 122: www.stockhausen.org

Page 133: Reich, Steve, *Writings on Music*, 1965–2000, Oxford University Press, 2002

Page 145: *John Tavener: A Portrait*, Naxos 8.558152–53, 2004

A Timeline of the Twentieth Century

	Music	History
1881	Bartók born	
1882	Kodály born; Wagner *Parsifal*	British suppression of nationalist rising in Egypt
1883	Varèse born; Webern born	
1884		Berlin Conference decides colonial divisions in Africa
1885	Berg born	Benz and Daimler develop first internal combustion engine
1886		Liberal government tries to pass Home Rule Bill for Ireland; gold found in Transvaal
1887	Verdi *Otello*	Emile Berliner makes first records using discs rather than cylinders

Art and Architecture	Literature
Picasso born	Dostoevsky dies; P.G. Wodehouse born; James *The Portrait of a Lady*
Braque born	Trollope dies; Joyce born; Virginia Woolf born
Manet dies	Marx dies; Nietzsche *Also sprach Zarathustra*
Modigliani born	Twain *The Adventures of Huckleberry Finn*
	Hugo dies; D.H. Lawrence born; Zola *Germinal*
Kokoshka born; last exhibition by the Impressionists	Hardy *The Mayor of Casterbridge*
Chagall born; Schwitters born	

	Music	History
1888		
1889		Universal Exhibition in Paris; Eiffel Tower built; British South Africa Company chartered
1890		London's first underground railway opens
1891	Prokofiev born	
1892	Milhaud born	
1893	Tchaikovsky Symphony No. 6	Henry Ford builds his first car; Keir Hardie founds Independent Labour Party in Britain; women granted the vote in New Zealand
1894	Debussy *Prélude à l'après-midi d'un faune*	accession of Tsar Nicholas II in Russia; Dreyfus wrongly convicted of treason in France
1895		Lumière brothers invent cinematograph
1896	Puccini *La Bohème*	Henri Becquerel discovers radioactivity
1897	Brahms dies; Dukas *The Sorcerer's Apprentice*	Britain conquers Sudan

Art and Architecture	Literature
Van Gogh settles in Arles	T.S. Eliot born; Raymond Chandler born; Kipling *Plain Tales from the Hills*
Van Gogh *Starry Night*	Browning dies; Hopkins dies
Van Gogh dies; Schiele born	Ibsen *Hedda Gabler*
Max Ernst born	Melville dies; Rimbaud dies; Wilde *The Picture of Dorian Gray*
	Tennyson dies
Miró born; Munch *The Scream*	
	Aldous Huxley born; Kipling *The Jungle Book*
Rodin *The Burghers of Calais*	Chekhov *The Seagull*; Hardy *Jude the Obscure*
	F. Scott Fitzgerald born; Housman *A Shropshire Lad*
Charles Rennie Mackintosh founds Glasgow School of Art	Rostand *Cyrano de Bergerac*

	Music	History
1898	Gershwin born; Strauss *Ein Heldenleben*	Spanish–American War: Cuba gains independence; Puerto Rico and Philippines ceded to USA
1899	Poulenc born; Sibelius Symphony No. 1; Schoenberg *Verklärte Nacht*	Boer War begins in South Africa
1900	Copland born; Puccini *Tosca;* Debussy *Nocturnes*	build-up of German sea power begins
1901	Verdi dies; Ravel *Jeux d'eau*	Queen Victoria dies; Marconi makes first transatlantic radio transmissions
1902	Walton born; Mahler Symphony No. 5; Debussy *Pelléas et Mélisande*	
1903	Wolf dies; Janáček *Jenůfa*	Wright brothers make first successful flight in America; Emmeline Pankhurst founds Women's Social and Political Union
1904	Puccini *Madama Butterfly;* Mahler *Kindertotenlieder*	
1905	Tippett born; Strauss *Salome;* Debussy *La Mer*	Bloody Sunday, St Petersburg: troops fire on workers
1906	Shostakovich born; Schoenberg Chamber Symphony No. 1	Dreyfus retried, found not guilty of treason (France); first Russian parliament

Magritte born; Henry Moore born	Mallarmé dies; Hemingway born; Wells *The War of the Worlds*
	Mallarmé *Poésies*
Picasso moves from Barcelona to Paris	Nietzsche dies; Wilde dies; Freud *The Interpretation of Dreams*
Toulouse-Lautrec dies; beginning of Picasso's Blue Period	Chekhov *Three Sisters*
	Zola dies; Conrad *Heart of Darkness*; James *The Wings of the Dove*
Gauguin dies; Pissarro dies; Rothko born	Orwell born; Waugh born
Dalí born	Chekhov *The Cherry Orchard*; Chekhov dies; Conrad *Nostromo*
exhibition in Paris by the Fauves ('Wild Beasts'); Derain *Boats in Collioure*	
Cézanne dies; Matisse *The Happiness of Life*; Picasso *Portrait of Gertrude Stein*	Ibsen dies; Beckett born; Barrie *Peter Pan*; Galsworthy *The Man of Property*

	Music	History
1907	Rachmaninov Symphony No. 2	Hague peace conference fails to secure arms limitation from Germany; Britain, France and Russia join to form the Triple Entente
1908	Rimsky-Korsakov dies; Carter born; Messiaen born; Elgar Symphony No. 1; Scriabin *Le Poème de l'extase*; Webern *Passacaglia*	Austria annexes Bosnia and Herzegovina; old age pension plan introduced in Britain by Asquith
1909	Albéniz dies; Mahler Symphony No. 9; Mahler *Das Lied von der Erde*; Rachmaninov Piano Concerto No. 3; Schoenberg Five Orchestral Pieces, Op. 16	Blériot flies across English Channel; first appearance in Paris of Diaghilev's Ballets Russes
1910	Strauss *Der Rosenkavalier*; Stravinsky *The Firebird*; Webern Five Pieces	Union of South Africa formed
1911	Mahler dies; Sibelius Symphony No. 4; Strauss *Der Rosenkavalier*; Stravinsky *Petrushka*; Bartók *Bluebeard's Castle*	Parliament Act (Britain) reduces power of House of Lords; National Insurance Act passed
1912	Cage born; Schoenberg *Pierrot lunaire*; Ravel *Daphnis et Chloé*; Ives *Three Places in New England*	first Balkan War; *Titanic* sinks on maiden voyage
1913	Britten born; Lutosł awski born; Stravinsky *The Rite of Spring*	new state of Albania created
1914		Archduke Franz Ferdinand of Austria assassinated; World War I begins

Art and Architecture	Literature
Picasso *Les Demoiselles d'Avignon*; beginning of Cubism	Auden born
Klimt *The Kiss*	Forster *A Room with a View*
Francis Bacon born; Futurist movement arises in Italy	
Matisse *La Danse* and *La Musique*	Tolstoy dies; Mark Twain dies
exhibition in Munich of Blaue Reiter group	Tennessee Williams born
Jackson Pollock born	Mann *Death in Venice*; Shaw *Pygmalion*
	Camus born; Lawrence *Sons and Lovers*
Kokoshka *Tempest*	Joyce *Dubliners*

	Music	History
1915	Scriabin dies; Berg Three Pieces for Orchestra, Op. 6	ill-fated landing by allied forces at Gallipoli
1916	Holst *The Planets*	battle of the Somme; beginning of Arab revolt against Turkish rule; Einstein theory of general relativity
1917	Satie *Parade*	USA enters war against Germany; Russian Revolution; Britain pledges support for Jewish homeland in Palestine
1918	Debussy dies; Bernstein born	World War I ends; fall of Austro-Hungarian Empire; influenza pandemic
1919	Bartók *The Miraculous Mandarin*	Treaty of Versailles, imposing heavy reparations on Germany
1920		prohibition introduced in USA
1921	Janáček *Kát'a Kabanová*; Vaughan Williams Symphony No. 3 'Pastoral'	Irish Free State established
1922	Xenakis born	Greeks expelled from Turkey; Mussolini establishes Fascism in Italy
1923	Stravinsky *Les Noces*; Berg *Wozzeck*	France occupies Ruhr

Art and Architecture	Literature
Gaudier-Brzeska dies; Dada founded in Zurich and New York	Buchan *The Thirty-Nine Steps*
	Henry James dies; Kafka *Metamorphosis*
Degas dies; Rodin dies	
Klimt dies; Schiele *The Family*; Schiele dies	Wilfred Owen dies; Apollinaire dies; Strachey *Eminent Victorians*
Renoir dies; Schwitters *Das Unbild*; Bauhaus founded by Walter Gropius	
Modigliani dies	Lawrence *Women in Love*; Wharton *The Age of Innocence*
Picasso *Mother and Child* and *Three Musicians*	Pirandello *Six Characters in Search of an Author*
Klee *The Twittering Machine*	Proust dies; Larkin born; T.S. Eliot *The Waste Land*; Galsworthy *The Forsyte Saga*; Joyce's *Ulysses* published in Paris
	Masefield *Collected Poems*

	Music	History
1924	Sibelius Symphony No. 7; Gershwin *Rhapsody in Blue*; Poulenc *Les Biches*	
1925	Boulez born	Germany joins League of Nations
1926	Kodály *Háry János*	General Strike in Britain
1927	Stravinsky *Oedipus Rex*	
1928	Janáček dies; Stockhausen born	
1929		stock market crashes on Wall Street, New York
1930	Stravinsky *Symphony of Psalms*	
1931	Nielsen dies; Walton *Belshazzar's Feast*	world slump and financial crisis
1932	Shostakovich *Lady Macbeth of the Mtsensk District*	world economic conference fails; Japan leaves League of Nations
1933	Górecki born; Penderecki born	Hitler becomes Chancellor of Germany, establishes Nazi rule
1934	Elgar dies; Delius dies; Holst dies; Birtwistle born; Maxwell Davies born	Germany leaves League of Nations, repudiates Treaty of Versailles and begins to rearm

Surrealism founded in Paris	Conrad dies; Kafka dies; Mann *The Magic Mountain*; Wodehouse *The Inimitable Jeeves*
Rauschenberg born: Picasso *Still Life with Antique Head*	Fitzgerald *The Great Gatsby*
Gaudí dies; Monet dies	Rilke dies
Warhol born	Woolf *To the Lighthouse*
	Hardy dies; Waugh *Decline and Fall*
Oldenburg born	Faulkner *The Sound and the Fury*
Jasper Johns born; Empire State Building begun, New York	Lawrence dies; Auden *Poems*
Alexander Calder creates his first mobiles	Woolf *The Waves*
	Huxley *Brave New World*
Bauhaus closed by Nazis	Yeats *Collected Poems*
	W. Carlos Williams *Collected Poems*

	Music	History
1935	Sallinen born; Pärt born; Berg Violin Concerto; Berg dies; Gershwin *Porgy and Bess*; Walton Symphony No. 1	Mussolini attacks Abyssinia
1936	Reich born	Hitler reoccupies Rhineland; Spanish Civil War begins
1937	Ravel dies; Gershwin dies; Glass born	
1938	Hindemith *Mathis der Maler*	Hitler annexes Austria; declaration of peaceful intent at Munich
1939	Tippett Concerto for Double String Orchestra	Freud dies; Hitler invades Czechoslovakia, then Poland; World War II begins
1940	Britten *Sinfonia da Requiem*	defeat of France; Churchill becomes British Prime Minister
1941	Messiaen *Quatuor pour le fin du temps*; Shostakovich Symphony No. 7; Tippett *A Child of Our Time*	Hitler invades USSR; Japanese attack on Pearl Harbor
1942	Britten *Hymn to St Cecilia*	Germans defeated at Stalingrad; Japanese take Singapore
1943	Bartók *Concerto for Orchestra*	Allied armies invade Italy
1944	Tavener born; Copland *Appalachian Spring*	Allied landings in Normandy

Art and Architecture	Literature
	Canetti *Auto-da-fé*
	Eliot *Collected Poems 1909–35*; Mitchell *Gone with the Wind*
Hockney born; Picasso paints gigantic mural *Guernica* for Paris world exhibition	Barrie dies; Wharton dies
Chagall *White Crucifixion*	Du Maurier *Rebecca*
	Yeats dies; Steinbeck *The Grapes of Wrath*
Klee dies	Hemingway *For Whom the Bell Tolls*
	Joyce dies; Woolf dies; O'Neill *Long Day's Journey into Night*
Edward Hopper *Nighthawks*	
Munch dies; Kandinsky dies; Mondrian dies	T.S. Eliot *Four Quartets*

	Music	History
1945	Bartók dies; Webern dies; Britten *Peter Grimes*	Germany surrenders; signing of UN charter; US drops atom bombs on Hiroshima and Nagasaki; Japan surrenders
1946		
1947	John Adams born	India and Pakistan become two separate and independent nations
1948	Strauss *Four Last Songs*; Messiaen *Turangalîla-symphonie*	state of Israel founded
1949	Strauss dies	NATO founded
1950		Korean War begins
1951	Schoenberg dies; Britten *Billy Budd*; Stravinsky *The Rake's Progress*	Festival of Britain; European Coal and Steel Community founded
1952	Tippett *The Midsummer Marriage*	Mau Mau rebellion, Kenya
1953	Prokofiev dies; Shostakovich Symphony No. 10; Stockhausen *Kontra-Punkte*	Stalin dies; Elizabeth II crowned queen
1954	Ives dies; Britten *The Turn of the Screw*; Varèse *Déserts*	British troops withdraw from Egypt; beginning of war in Vietnam

Art and Architecture	Literature
	Henry Green *Loving*; Orwell *Animal Farm*
	Wells dies; Kazantzakis *Zorba the Greek*
Pierre Bonnard dies; Matisse *Jazz*; Le Corbusier begins design of Unité d'Habitation, Marseilles	Camus *The Plague*; Levi *If This is a Man*
Schwitters dies	Betjeman *Selected Poems*
	Miller *Death of a Salesman*; Orwell *Nineteen Eighty-Four*
Picasso *Portrait of a Painter, after El Greco*	Orwell dies; Shaw dies; Greene *The Third Man*
	Salinger *The Catcher in the Rye*
	Beckett *Waiting for Godot*; Fleming *Casino Royale*
Matisse dies; Mies van der Rohe begins building Seagram Building, New York	Amis *Lucky Jim*; Golding *Lord of the Flies*

	Music	History
1955		Warsaw Pact
1956	Bernstein *Candide*; Carter *Variations for Orchestra*	British and French invade Suez
1957	Sibelius dies; Bernstein *West Side Story*; Poulenc *Les Dialogues des Carmélites*	Treaty of Rome establishes European Economic Community
1958	Vaughan Williams dies; Cage *Fontana Mix*; Messiaen *Catalogue d'oiseaux*	
1959		Cuban Revolution
1960	Boulez *Pli selon pli*	15 African nations achieve independence
1961	Britten *War Requiem*; Henze *Elegy for Young Lovers*; Tippett *King Priam*	Berlin Wall built; USSR puts first man into space orbit
1962		Cuban missile crisis
1963	Poulenc dies	Kennedy assassinated in Dallas
1964	Britten *Curlew River*; Riley *In C*	Civil Rights Act, USA
1965	Varèse dies	Churchill dies; US troops sent to Vietnam

Art and Architecture	Literature
	Tolkien *The Lord of the Rings*
Jackson Pollock dies	Osborne *Look Back in Anger*
Brancusi dies; Jorn Utzon begins work on the Opera House, Sydney	Pasternak *Doctor Zhivago*; Patrick White *Voss*
Rauschenberg *Talisman*	Greene *Our Man in Havana*
Stanley Spencer dies; Rothko *Red on Maroon*	Grass *The Tin Drum*
	Pasternak dies; Pinter *The Caretaker*
Augustus John dies; 'Young Contemporaries' exhibition, London	Hemingway dies; Heller *Catch-22*
Warhol becomes leading figure in Pop Art; Oldenburg *Dual Hamburger The Golden Notebook*	Albee *Who's Afraid of Virginia Woolf?*; Lessing *The Golden Notebook*
Braque dies	Frost dies; Huxley dies
	T.S. Eliot dies

	Music	History
1966	Berio *Sequenza III*; Penderecki *St Luke Passion*	Cultural Revolution begins, China
1967	Kodály dies; Takemitsu *November Steps*	Israel wins Six Day War; Abortion Act, Britain
1968	Birtwistle *Punch and Judy*; Stockhausen *Stimmung*	Prague Spring: USSR invades Czechoslovakia; Martin Luther King assassinated
1969	Maxwell Davies *Eight Songs for a Mad King*	first manned landing on moon
1970	Crumb *Ancient Voices of Children*; Ferneyhough *Cassandra's Dream Song*	
1971	Stravinsky dies	microprocessor developed
1972	Reich *Drumming*; Tippett Symphony No. 3	Watergate scandal begins to unfold, USA; terrorist attack at Olympic Games, Munich
1973	Britten *Death in Venice*	USA withdraws from Vietnam; Britain enters European Economic Community
1974	Milhaud dies	Nixon resigns as US president; Turkey invades Cyprus

Carl André *Equivalent VIII* (using bricks)	Waugh dies; Fowles *The Magus*
Magritte dies	Márquez *One Hundred Years of Solitude*; Stoppard *Rosencrantz and Guildenstern Are Dead*
	Steinbeck dies
Rothko dies; Sears Tower, Chicago begun (Skidmore, Owings and Merrill)	Forster dies
Pompidou Centre, Paris begun (Rogers and Piano); Cy Twombly *Nini's Painting*	Updike *Rabbit Redux*
Picasso dies	Auden dies

	Music	History
1975	Shostakovich dies; Boulez *Rituel in Memoriam Maderna*; Ligeti *San Francisco Polyphony*	civil war begins, Lebanon; Pol Pot becomes dictator of Cambodia; Microsoft founded
1976	Britten dies; Glass *Einstein on the Beach*; Górecki Symphony No. 3; Pärt *Cantus in Memoriam Benjamin Britten*	unification of South and North Vietnam
1977	Reich *Music for 18 Musicians*	
1978		revolution in Iran; John Paul II becomes Pope
1979	Tippett Triple Concerto	Margaret Thatcher becomes British Prime Minister
1980	Lutosławski Double Concerto	Solidarity founded, Poland
1981	Barber dies	first space shuttle flight; AIDS diagnosed
1982		Britain and Argentina at war over Falkland Islands/Malvinas
1983	Walton dies; Messiaen *St Francis of Assisi*	
1984	Glass *Akhnaten*; Tippett *The Mask of Time*	Indira Gandhi assassinated, India

Art and Architecture	Literature
Barbara Hepworth dies	Wodehouse dies; Bradbury *The History Man*; Paul Scott *A Division of the Spoils* (last of *Raj Quartet*)
Max Ernst dies	
Pompidou Centre opens; Anthony Caro *Emma Dipper*	Nabokov dies
	Murdoch *The Sea, the Sea*
	Golding *Darkness Visible*
Kokoshka dies	Sartre dies; Eco *The Name of the Rose*
	Rushdie *Midnight's Children*
	Boyd *An Ice-Cream War*; Alice Walker *The Color Purple*
Miró dies	Tennessee Williams dies
	Betjeman dies; Kundera *The Unbearable Lightness of Being*; Martin Amis *Money*

	Music	History
1985	Ligeti *Études pour piano*, Book 1; Maxwell Davies Symphony No. 3; Takemitsu *Riverrun*	Ethiopian famine
1986	Nyman *The Man who Mistook his Wife for a Hat*; Schnittke Violin Concerto	President Marcos overthrown, Philippines; USA bombs Libya
1987	Adams *Nixon in China*	
1988	Turnage *Greek*	
1989	Berio *Rendering*; Tavener *The Protecting Veil*	Romanian revolution; Berlin Wall destroyed; Tiananmen Square massacre, Beijing
1990	Copland dies; Bernstein dies; Adams *The Death of Klinghoffer*	Iraq invades Kuwait; Germany reunified; Nelson Mandela released from prison
1991	Birtwistle *Gawain*	USSR dissolved; UN forces attack Iraq
1992	Cage dies; Messiaen dies; Henze Requiem	end of Cold War
1993	Tavener *Song for Athene*	
1994	Lutosł awski dies	Mandela first president of multiracial democracy, South Africa; genocide begins in Rwanda; Channel Tunnel opens

Chagall dies; Jeff Koons *One Ball Total Equilibrium Tank*; Saatchi Gallery opens, London	Graves dies; Larkin dies
Henry Moore dies	
Warhol dies	McEwan *The Child in Time*
	Raymond Carver *Where I'm Calling From*; Margaret Atwood *Cat's Eye*
Dalí dies	Beckett dies; Ishiguro *The Remains of the Day*; Anne Tyler *Breathing Lessons*
	Patrick White dies
Damien Hirst *The Physical Impossibility of Death in the Mind of Someone Living* (shark piece)	Greene dies; Angela Carter *Wise Children*
Francis Bacon dies; Rachel Whiteread *Untitled (House)*	Ondaatje *The English Patient*
	Golding dies; Stoppard *Arcadia*
	Osborne dies

	Music	History
1995	Adès *Powder Her Face*	Yitzhak Rabin assassinated, Israel
1996	MacMillan *The World's Ransoming*; Turnage *Blood on the Floor*	
1997	Harvey Percussion Concerto; Rautavaara *Aleksis Kivi*	
1998	Tippett dies; Pärt *Kanon Pokajanen*	India and Pakistan test nuclear weapons
1999		NATO forces attack Serbia; introduction of euro as common currency in EU
2000	Adams *El Niño*; Maxwell Davies *Antarctica Symphony*	
2001	Xenakis dies	attack on World Trade Center

Bill Viola *The Greeting* (video); Museum of Contemporary Art, Barcelona completed (Richard Meier)	Carol Shields *The Stone Diaries*
	Byatt *Babel Tower*, Graham Swift *Last Orders*
Guggenheim Bilbao completed (Frank O. Gehry)	Laurie Lee dies; DeLillo *Underworld*; McEwan *Enduring Love*; Ted Hughes *Tales from Ovid*
	Hughes dies; Murdoch dies; Roth *American Pastoral*
Tate Modern opens, London; Jake and Dinos Chapman *Hell*	Atwood *The Blind Assassin*; Roth *The Human Stain*

Composers of the 20th Century

John Adams (1947–)
(*b.* Worcester, MA, USA)

Thomas Adès (1971–)
(*b.* London, England)

Louis Andriessen (1939–)
(*b.* Utrecht, The Netherlands)

Sir Malcolm Arnold (1921–2006)
(*b.* Northampton, England; *d.* Norwich, England)

Georges Auric (1899–1983)
(*b.* Lodève, France; *d.* Paris, France)

Samuel Barber (1910–1981)
(*b.* West Chester, PA, USA; *d.* New York, USA)

Béla Bartók (1881–1945)
(*b.* Nagyszentmiklós, Hungary [now Sînnicolau Mare, Romania]; *d.* New York, USA)

Sir Richard Rodney Bennett (1936–)
(*b.* Broadstairs, England)

Alban Berg (1885–1935)
(*b.* Vienna, Austria; *d.* Vienna, Austria)

Luciano Berio (1925–2003)
(*b.* Oneglia, Italy; *d.* Rome, Italy)

Leonard Bernstein (1918–1990)
(*b.* Lawrence, MA, USA; *d.* New York, USA)

Sir Harrison Birtwistle (1934–)
(*b.* Accrington, England)

Marc Blitzstein (1905–1964)
(*b.* Philadelphia, USA; *d.* Fort-de-France, Martinique)

Pierre Boulez (1925–)
(*b.* Montbrison, France)

Benjamin Britten (1913–1976)
(*b.* Lowestoft, England; *d.* Aldeburgh, England)

Gavin Bryars (1943–)
(*b.* Goole, England)

George Butterworth (1885–1916)
(*b.* London, England; *d.* Pozières, France)

John Cage (1912–1992)
(*b.* Los Angeles, CA, USA; *d.* New York, USA)

Elliott Carter (1908–)
(*b.* New York, USA)

Aaron Copland (1900–1990)
(*b.* Brooklyn, NY, USA; *d.* North Tarrytown, NY, USA)

John Corigliano (1938–)
(*b.* New York, USA)

Claude Debussy (1862–1918)
(*b.* St Germain-en-Laye, France; *d.* Paris, France)

Louis Durey (1888–1979)
(*b.* Paris, France; *d.* Saint-Tropez, France)

Sir Edward Elgar (1857–1934)
(*b.* Broadheath, England; *d.* Worcester, England)

Manuel de Falla (1876–1946)
(*b.* Cádiz, Spain; *d.* Alta Gracia, Argentina)

Morton Feldman (1926–1987)
(*b.* New York, USA; *d.* Buffalo, NY, USA)

Brian Ferneyhough (1943–)
(*b.* Coventry, England)

Michael Finnissy (1946–)
(*b.* London, England)

Gerald Finzi (1901–1956)
(*b.* London, England; *d.* Oxford, England)

George Gershwin (1898–1937)
(*b.* Brooklyn, NY, USA; *d.* Hollywood, CA, USA)

Philip Glass (1937–)
(*b.* Baltimore, MD, USA)

Alexander Goehr (1932–)
(*b.* Berlin, Germany)

Henryk Górecki (1933–)
(*b.* Czernica, Poland)

Roy Harris (1898–1979)
(*b.* Chandler, OK, USA; *d.* Santa Monica, CA, USA)

Hans Werner Henze (1926–)
(*b.* Gütersloh, Germany)

Paul Hindemith (1895–1963)
(*b.* Hanau, Germany; *d.* Frankfurt, Germany)

Gustav Holst (1874–1934)
(*b.* Cheltenham, England; *d.* London, England)

Arthur Honegger (1892–1955)
(*b.* Le Havre, France; *d.* Paris, France)

Charles Ives (1874–1954)
(*b.* Danbury, CT, USA; *d.* New York, USA)

Leoš Janáček (1854–1928)
(*b.* Hukvaldy, Moravia [now Czech Republic]; *d.* Moravská Ostrava, Moravia)

Zoltán Kodály (1882–1967)
(*b.* Kecskemét, Hungary; *d.* Budapest, Hungary)

Helmut Lachenmann (1935–2006)
(*b.* Stuttgart, Germany)

György Ligeti (1923–)
(*b.* Dicsöszentmárton, Transylvania [now Tîrnăveni, Romania];
d. Vienna, Austria)

Magnus Lindberg (1958–)
(*b.* Helsinki, Finland)

Witold Lutosławski (1913–1994)
(*b.* Warsaw, Poland; *d.* Warsaw, Poland)

Bruno Maderna (1920–1973)
(*b.* Venice, Italy; *d.* Darmstadt, Germany)

Sir Peter Maxwell Davies (1934–)
(*b.* Salford, England)

James MacMillan (1959–)
(*b.* Kilwinning, Scotland)

Olivier Messiaen (1908–1992)
(*b.* Avignon, France; *d.* Paris, France)

Darius Milhaud (1892–1974)
(*b.* Marseille, France; *d.* Geneva, Switzerland)

Carl Nielsen (1865–1931)
(*b.* Sortelung, Denmark; *d.* Copenhagen, Denmark)

Luigi Nono (1924–1990)
(*b.* Venice, Italy; *d.* Venice, Italy)

Per Nørgård (1932–)
(*b.* Gentofte, Denmark)

Michael Nyman (1944–)
(*b.* London, England)

Arvo Pärt (1935–)
(*b.* Paide, Estonia)

Krzysztof Penderecki (1933–)
(*b.* Dębica, Poland)

Francis Poulenc (1899–1963)
(*b.* Paris, France; *d.* Paris, France)

Sergey Prokofiev (1891–1953)
(*b.* Sontsovka, Russia; *d.* Moscow, Russia)

Sergey Rachmaninov (1873–1943)
(*b.* Oneg, Russia; *d.* Beverly Hills, CA, USA)

Maurice Ravel (1875–1937)
(*b.* Ciboure, France; *d.* Paris, France)

Steve Reich (1936–)
(*b.* New York, USA)

Terry Riley (1935–)
(*b.* Colfax, CA, USA)

Poul Ruders (1949–)
(*b.* Ringsted, Denmark)

Kaija Saariaho (1952–)
(*b.* Helsinki, Finland)

Aulis Sallinen (1935–)
(*b.* Salmi, Finland [now Russia])

Erik Satie (1866–1925)
(*b.* Honfleur, France; *d.* Paris, France)

Alfred Schnittke (1934–1998)
(*b.* Engels, Russia; *d.* Hamburg, Germany)

Arnold Schoenberg (1874–1951)
(*b.* Vienna, Austria; *d.* Los Angeles, CA, USA)

Dmitry Shostakovich (1906–1975)
(*b.* St Petersburg, Russia; *d.* Moscow, Russia)

Jean Sibelius (1865–1957)
(*b.* Hämeenlinna, Finland; *d.* Järvenpää, Finland)

Karlheinz Stockhausen (1928–2007)
(*b.* Mödrath, Germany; *d.* Köln, Germany)

Richard Strauss (1864–1949)
(*b.* Munich, Germany; *d.* Garmisch-Partenkirchen, Germany)

Igor Stravinsky (1882–1971)
(*b.* Oranienbaum [now Lomonosov], Russia; *d.* New York, USA)

Tōru Takemitsu (1930–1996)
(*b.* Tokyo, Japan; *d.* Tokyo, Japan)

Germaine Tailleferre (1892–1983)
(*b.* Parc-St-Maur, France; *d.* Paris, France)

John Tavener (1944–)
(*b.* London, England)

Virgil Thomson (1896–1989)
(*b.* Kansas City, MO, USA; *d.* New York, USA)

Sir Michael Tippett (1905–1998)
(*b.* London, England; *d.* London, England)

Edgard Varèse (1883–1965)
(*b.* Paris, France; *d.* New York, USA)

Ralph Vaughan Williams (1872–1958)
(*b.* Down Ampney, England; *d.* London, England)

William Walton (1902–1983)
(*b.* Oldham, England; *d.* Ischia, Italy)

Peter Warlock (1894–1930)
(*b.* London, England; *d.* London, England)

Anton Webern (1883–1945)
(*b.* Vienna, Austria; *d.* Mittersill, Austria)

John Williams (1932–)
(*b.* New York, USA)

Iannis Xenakis (1922–2001)
(*b.* Braïla, Romania; *d.* Paris, France)

La Monte Young (1935–)
(*b.* Bern, ID, USA)

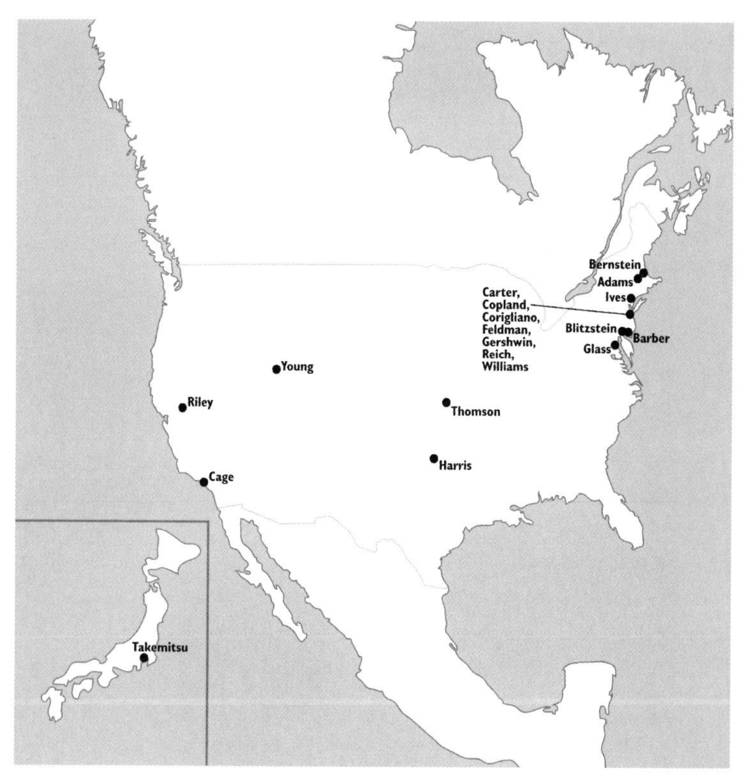

maps showing birthplaces of twentieth-century composers

Rachmaninov
Sallinen
Sibelius
Shostakovich
Stravinsky
Lindberg,
Saariaho
Pärt
Schnittke
Adès,
Nyman,
Butterworth,
Finnissy,
Finzi,
Tavener,
Tippett,
Warlock
Birtwistle
Walton,
Maxwell Davies
MacMillan
Nielsen
Nørgård
Ruders
Elgar
Bryars
Ferneyhough
Britten
Lutosławski
Goehr
Henze
Arnold
Andriessen
Górecki
Prokofiev
Holst
Stockhausen
Penderecki
Bennett
Hindemith
Janáček
Vaughan Williams
Lachenmann
Satie
Berg,
Schoenberg,
Webern
R. Strauss
Kodály
Ligeti
Honegger
Tailleferre
Bartók
Xenakis
Debussy
Nono, Maderna
Durey,
Poulenc,
Varèse
Boulez
Berio
Messiaen
Ravel
Auric
Milhaud
Falla

Glossary

A cappella music written for choir without instrumental accompaniment

Adagio slow

Aleatoric music see 'indeterminacy'

Atonal descriptive of music which is not in a key (see also 'tonality')

Avant garde French term referring to experimental art. It derives from the military practice of sending an advance guard ahead of a large army to explore the terrain. In twentieth-century music the term generally refers to the innovative movement of the 1950s and 1960s spearheaded by Stockhausen and Boulez in Europe, and Cage in the USA.

Baroque era the period of Western classical music from roughly 1600 to 1750

Bass the lowest form of male voice, the term is also used to describe the lowest part (or less specifically the lowest register) in any chord or piece

Blues a type of American popular music which emerged in the late nineteenth and early twentieth century. The form grew out of African-American work songs and spirituals.

Brass the family of instruments (e.g. the French horn, trumpet, trombone, tuba) which, as the term suggests, are made out of brass

Chamber music music for small groups of players, such as a string quartet or a piano trio – so called because such music was originally played in the 'chamber' or home

Chance music see 'indeterminacy'

Choreographer the person who creates the steps and movement for a dance production, such as a ballet

Chromatic (chromaticism) notes (and the using of notes) which are not contained in the standard 'diatonic' scales forming the basis of most Western tonal music. On the piano, for example, the scale of C major uses only the white keys; every black note is therefore 'chromatic'.

Cimbalom an instrument of the Hungarian gypsies, with a distinctive plangent and exotic sound. It is made of wood with strings which are struck by a mallet covered in cotton, wool or leather.

Classical era the period of Western classical music from roughly 1750 to 1830

Collage a term borrowed from the visual arts, which refers to a technique in which a composer creates a piece by superimposing several tunes, passages or styles on top of each other

Colour the darkness or brightness of the sound of one or more instruments and/or voices

Concerto A work for solo (or occasionally more than one) instrument and orchestra, traditionally in three movements (fast–slow–fast)

Concerto grosso an important musical form of the Baroque era, in which the musical material passes between a small group of solo instruments (the *concertino*) and the main orchestra (the *ripieno*). The concerto grosso usually consists of four to six movements.

Dissonance opposite of 'consonance'; descriptive of the grating or 'unresolved' sound produced by a chord or combination of notes which causes a harmonic clash

Dodecaphonic music see 'serialism'

Dynamics the gradations of softness and loudness, and the terms that indicate them

Edison wax cylinder one of the earliest pieces of recording equipment, developed in the 1880s by Thomas Edison. The sound recording was etched into a rotating cylinder made of slightly soft wax. Due to the lack of durability of the wax, the recording would often wear out after it had been played back twenty or thirty times.

Electronic music traditionally, music created exclusively by electronic means, without the use of any natural sounds. Electronic music grew out of the research of the post-Webern generation of composers in the 1950s. See also 'musique concrète'.

Ethnomusicology the study of traditional music outside the Western art tradition

Expressionism the intensification of expression, in which turbulence and chaos are predominant

Fantasia a free form, often of an improvisatory nature, following the composer's whim rather than any preordained structures

Flamenco a traditional type of music from Southern Spain characterised by its distinctive rhythm and exotic-sounding scales. Lying half-way between folk music and art music, it is generally performed by specially trained singers to a guitar accompaniment.

Forlane a lighthearted dance in triple metre (each beat is subdivided into three) that originated in northern Italy in the sixteenth century and became popular with Baroque composers

Fugue a piece which is built entirely around imitative counterpoint (the interweaving of separate horizontal lines). A fugue will usually consist of three or four instrumental or vocal strands (known as voices); it is based on a short tune (called the subject or theme) which is stated at the beginning by a single voice, and then taken up by the other voices and repeated in quick succession throughout the whole piece.

Gamelan a traditional Indonesian orchestra consisting mainly of percussion instruments such as gongs, drums, metallophones and xylophones. The exotic sound of the gamelan has inspired many Western composers throughout the twentieth century, including Debussy, Messiaen and Britten.

Hammond organ an electronic organ invented by Laurens Hammond in 1935. It was originally intended for church use, but became popular with jazz, blues, gospel and rock musicians.

Harmony the simultaneous sounding of notes to make a chord; harmonies (chords) often serve as an expressive or atmospheric 'adjectives', describing or giving added meaning to the notes of a melody

'Holy minimalism' a term used to describe the work of a group of composers whose compositions in a sparse, contemplative style are inspired by a deep religious faith. John Tavener and Arvo Pärt are famous protagonists.

I Ching an ancient system of cosmology and philosophy which is central to Chinese cultural beliefs. It consists of sixty-four interrelated hexagrams (originally used for divination) which embody Taoist philosophy by describing the universe in terms of interaction of yin and yang.

Impressionism a term borrowed from French painting to describe the fluid, progressive music being written by composers such as Debussy at the end of the nineteenth century

Indeterminacy also called chance music or aleatoric music; an avant-garde musical technique which leaves some of the elements of the piece to chance. The chance can occur at the time of composition, as in Cage's *Music of Changes*, in which the composer determined elements such as tempo, note durations and dynamics by note durations and dynamics by throwing dice; or the chance can be left to the time of performance, such as in Stockhausen's *Zyklus* (1959) for percussion – here the player can choose to read the spiral-bound score from any point clockwise, anti-clockwise or even upside down.

Jazz a type of indigenous American music that originated in New Orleans in around 1900, characterised by syncopated rhythms and improvisation. Jazz grew out of the American minstrel-show music, ragtime, early brass and early string bands.

Key Denotes the relationships between pitches that establish a tone as tonal centre or tonic. The key of a work (or part of a work) is either major or minor depending on the scale from which the notes are drawn. The home key is the one in which a piece of tonal music starts and finishes. (See also 'tonality'.)

Ländler an Austrian dance with three beats in a bar, like a slow waltz

Leitmotif compositional device – developed mostly by Wagner in his operas and music dramas – in which a theme is used recurrently to identify and amplify a character, situation or object

Libretto the text of an opera or an oratorio

Major see 'mode'

Menuet also minuet; originally a French dance, in the folk tradition, it can be seen as an ancestor of the waltz: both have three beats in a bar and also an elegance from being performed and developed over years in Europe's royal courts

Metronome a device which indicates the speed at which music should be played, by producing a clicking sound either by use of a pendulum or, as is more common nowadays, by electronic means

Micropolyphony a dense form of polyphony (music with two or more interweaving strands) in which clusters of many overlapping motifs create a complex texture of harmonies which do not change clearly but merge seamlessly into one another

Minimalism dating from the 1960s, a musical technique in which composers built up entire pieces out of the repetition in regular rhythm of chords or simple motifs

Minor see 'mode'

Mode the name given to a particular arrangement of notes within a scale; every key in Western classical music has two versions, the major and the minor mode; the decisive factor is the size of the interval between the key note (the tonic) and the third degree of the scale; if it is compounded of two whole tones (as in C–E), the mode is major; if only one and a half tones (C–E flat), the mode is minor. The minor mode tends to be darker and more dramatic than the major. The church modes prevalent in the Middle Ages, which comprise various combinations of major and minor, appear only rarely in music after the Baroque era and then usually to create some kind of archaic effect.

Motif a kind of musical acorn – a melodic/rhythmic figure too brief to constitute a proper theme, but one out of which themes are built. A perfect example is the beginning of Beethoven's Symphony No. 5: ta-ta-ta *dah*; ta-ta-ta *dah*.

Movement comparable to a chapter in a book; a primary, self-contained division of a larger work

Multimedia a work of art, or production that makes use of several different media, such as Philip Glass and Robert Wilson's collaborative work *Monsters of Grace*, which combines music, theatre and projected 3D digital animation

Musicology the academic and historical study of music

Musique concrète a form of electronic music produced by editing and electronically manipulating taped fragments of natural, instrumental and industrial sounds

Nationalism in music, nationalism refers to pieces that make use of traditional and folk music to instil a strong sense of patriotism. Nationalist music emerged in the middle of the nineteenth century, particularly in small Eastern and Central European countries as a reaction against the dominance of the Austro-Hungarian Empire in the region.

Neoclassicism musical movement which flourished in Paris in the 1920s and 1930s in which composers found inspiration in the formal techniques of earlier eras, most particularly the eighteenth century (the Classical era)

Neo-Romantic descriptive of music written in the twentieth and twenty-first centuries which has a lyricism and lushness of texture akin to that of the Romantic era (nineteenth century)

Noh drama traditional Japanese drama. Noh dramas are highly stylised and are accompanied by traditional Japanese music.

Note row see 'series'

Octave the musical interval of eight notes; an octave spans the first and last notes of a major or minor scale, beginning and ending on the same letter name

Ondes martenot an early electronic instrument with an other-worldly sound. Invented in 1928 by Maurice Martenot, it consists of a keyboard and a sliding ribbon which enables the instrument to slide between notes.

Opera basically, a sung play – a stage work which combines words, drama, music (with singers and orchestra) and often elaborate scenery

Oratorio an extended choral/orchestral setting of a religious text in a dramatic and semi-operatic fashion; the most famous example is Handel's *Messiah*

Orchestration the art of using instruments in the orchestra for specific expressive, dramatic, colouristic, structural and textural purposes; also, the arrangement for orchestra of works originally written for other media

Overture a single orchestral movement, normally designed to introduce an opera, oratorio or a play with music, and often based on the main themes of the following work. The term can also apply to a freestanding concert work, generally alluding in its title to a literary, pictorial or emotional theme, as in Mendelssohn's *The Hebrides*.

Passacaglia a musical dance form in triple metre, originating in the Baroque era, which contains a melody that is constantly repeated throughout. Famous examples include Bach's Passacaglia in C minor and 'Dido's Lament' (from Purcell's *Dido and Aeneas*).

Pastoral style a specifically 'English'-sounding musical style that was very popular with British composers, including Vaughan Williams, Finzi and Butterworth, in the first half of the twentieth century. It was characterised by the richness of its gentle yet rousing textures and harmonies, and often had the modal flavour of English folksongs.

Pentatonic scale a five-note scale (demonstrated by playing the black notes on a piano in sequence) that is found in much ethnic music from around the world. Debussy was the first Western composer to make significant use of this scale in his works.

Percussion family of instruments whose sound is produced by being beaten or struck by an object. Examples of percussion instruments include timpani, xylophone, marimba, drums, cymbal and triangle.

Phase music minimalist compositional technique invented by Steve Reich in the mid-1960s in which the same melody or phrase is played in two or more parts. The parts begin at the same time but proceed at slightly different speeds, increasingly losing synchronisation with each other in an ever-changing rhythmic and melodic pattern, until they eventually become synchronised again. Due to the absolute precision of tempo required in phase music, the parts are usually individually pre-recorded and played back on tape in performance.

Pitch the highness or lowness of a note in relation to other notes

Pizzicato plucked

Pluralism the simultaneous co-existence of many different styles

Pointillism a term originally associated with late-nineteenth- and early-twentieth-century visual art, in which artists created the impression of secondary colours by the juxtaposition of tiny dots of primary colours. In music, pointillism refers to the creation of a broader musical texture by the combination of many brief gestures played on different instruments.

Polytonality music that is in several keys at the same time

Post-Romanticism a fluid term which is used to describe music that lies somewhere between the idioms of the Romantic era and the more radical new styles of the twentieth century

Prelude literally, a piece that is heard first and introduces another piece (as in 'Prelude and Fugue'). It is also used for short, freestanding pieces.

Programme music music that is dependent on extra-musical sources, that is specifically designed to tell a story (as in Berlioz's *Symphonie fantastique*); see also 'tone poem'

Rap technique which emerged in pop music in the 1980s consisting of rhyming lyrics spoken rhythmically over instrumental music. Rap music is often associated with black urban culture.

Reggae musical style which was developed in Jamaica and entered the mainstream in the 1970s. Bob Marley is probably the most famous reggae artist of all time.

Requiem the Roman Catholic Mass for the dead. Many composers, including Berlioz, Brahms, Mozart, Britten and Penderecki, have written Requiems for concert and ceremonial use.

Rhythm the aspect of music concerned with duration and accent. Notes may be of many contrasting lengths and derive much of their character and definition from patterns of accentuation and emphasis determined by the composer.

Rigaudon a Baroque dance form, originating in Provence, that was commonly heard in the operatic ballets of Lully and Rameau

Ring modulator an electronic device, mostly used in synthesisers, which produces bell-like or other metallic sounds (e.g. in the theme music for the original *Dr Who* TV series in Britain)

Romantic era the era of Western classical music, roughly from 1830 to 1900

Score the sheet music, or written version of a piece of music, showing all the parts for the musicians

Second Viennese School A trio of composers – Schoenberg, Berg and Webern – who explored atonal and serial techniques of composition in Vienna in the early twentieth century

Semitone half a tone (C–C sharp; A flat–A); the smallest interval it is possible to show in standard Western musical notation. See also 'tone'.

Serialism also called dodecaphonic music and twelve-note music; compositional technique developed by Schoenberg which marked a major break with tonality – the backbone of Western music for 300 years – and which proved to be one of the most influential new techniques of the twentieth century. Serial music is based on a 'series' or 'row', in which all twelve notes in the chromatic scale appear in a particular order. After each note in the series is heard, it cannot be heard again until all other eleven notes in the series have been sounded. Notes can be played together in a chord, and the composer may also be creative with the row itself, using it in retrograde (backwards), inverted (upside down) or even retrograde inversion (upside down and backwards)

Series also called note row or tone row; in serialism, it is a sequence of twelve notes (or sequence of rhythms, dynamics, durations or articulations), each of which cannot be repeated until all the others have been heard

Sextet a piece of music for six instruments; an ensemble consisting of six musicians

Side drum also called snare drum; a small cylindrical drum with two heads stretched over a metal shell

Sine wave a wave form that is generated by a uniform frequency; the purest form of electronic sound, such as an ideal, unmodulated wireless signal, produces a sine waveform

Song cycle a sequence of accompanied songs, connected by a common subject. The cycle is often of a cumulatively narrative nature, with the poems generally being by a single poet.

Sprechgesang A vocal technique, famously used by Schoenberg in *Pierrot lunaire*, in which a text is half-sung, half-spoken and in which pitches are approximate

String quartet an ensemble consisting of two violins, viola and cello; or a piece of music written for such an ensemble

Suite an instrumental piece comprising several movements while not conforming to a fixed large-scale pattern as in the symphony or sonata. In the eighteenth century the term specifically denoted a sequence of dance movements but is now used to describe any fairly loose assemblage of movements, often from an opera, ballet, play or film.

Surrealism artistic movement that emerged in the 1920s which emphasised the workings of the subconscious and the imagination. Surrealist art, as exemplified by the works of the Spanish artist Salvador Dalí, is characterised by strange and fantastical imagery.

Symphony an extended piece of music for orchestra, generally comprising several movements. Twentieth-century symphonic structure was free and flexible, often far removed from the strict sonata form that was adhered to in the eighteenth century.

Theremin one of the earliest electronic instruments, invented in 1919 by the Russian, Lev Sergeyevich Termen. It consists of a box with two radio antennae attached. The box doesn't need to be touched for the instrument to be played – the perfomer's hands are simply moved in the air around the instrument to control the pitch and volume.

Thumb piano also called mbira; a traditional East African instrument, consisting of between 22 and 28 metal strips fixed to a soundboard which in turn is placed inside a resonator to amplify the sound. The instrument is played by brushing the metal strips either downwards or upwards with the fingers or thumbs. The resulting sound is somewhere between that of a marimba and a harp.

Timbre the particular quality of a sound made by an instrument or voice

Timpani also called kettledrums; belonging to the percussion family, each instrument consists of a skin stretched over a large copper bowl, and is played by striking the head with a stick. Unlike many other types of drum, timpani are tuned to a specific pitch.

Toccata a Baroque form which emerged at the end of the sixteenth century, a toccata was originally a piece for keyboard written in a free style which highlighted the performer's technical ability.

Tonality at its broadest, any musical system that has keys or modes at its core

Tone the interval of a major 2nd – the sum of two semitones, as in the first two notes of *Frère Jacques*; see also 'semitone'

Tone cluster literally, a cluster of tones – a simultaneous sounding of several closely spaced notes, producing a dissonant sound

Tone poem also known as symphonic poem, an orchestral form in which a poem or programme provides a narrative or illustrative basis

Tone row see 'series'

Twelve-note music see 'serialism'

Verbunkos a Hungarian dance and music genre, established in the eighteenth century. Originally, *verbunkos* music was played during military recruitment.

Waltz originally a popular ballroom dance in triple metre, it also exists in the form of 'concert' waltzes, such as those by Chopin and Brahms, which were never intended for actual dancing

White noise for the technically minded, a noise with a frequency spectrum that is uniform and continuous over a specified frequency band; for the non-technically minded, a 'shhh' noise, as produced by a radio or television tuned off-channel

Whole-tone scale a scale consisting of six whole-tone steps. Due to intervals between consecutive notes in the scale being the same, there is no sense of being in any one key. Debussy's pioneering use of this scale in his works challenged the idea that all Western music had to be tonal.

Woodwind family of instruments which were originally made of wood; all of them are blown to produce a sound.

World music music which is not part of the mainstream popular or classical tradition, and which has some ethnic component

About the Author

David McCleery studied music at Manchester University before embarking on a career in arts administration. After various jobs with orchestras, artists' agencies and festivals, he joined Chester Music and Novello music publishers where he developed a keen interest in working with composers, including John Tavener, Richard Rodney Bennett and Thea Musgrave. That interest continues today, although he has moved to the field of media music and works for a management company for film and television composers. When time permits, he undertakes freelance writing projects. For Naxos, he has written *A Portrait of John Tavener*, as well as *Discover Music of the Romantic Era*.

Photography Acknowledgements

Naxos would like to thank the following sources for photographs:

Claude Debussy: Lebrecht Music & Arts Photo Library
Richard Strauss: Universal Edition
Arnold Schoenberg: Universal Edition
Alban Berg: Universal Edition
Anton Webern: Universal Edition
Maurice Ravel: Lebrecht Music & Arts Photo Library
Igor Stravinsky: Boosey & Hawkes / Gene Fenn
Ralph Vaughan Williams: Boosey & Hawkes
Benjamin Britten: Boosey & Hawkes / Angus McBean
Leoš Janáček: Universal Edition
Zoltán Kodály: Universal Edition
Béla Bartók: Universal Edition
Sergey Prokofiev: Boosey & Hawkes
Dmitry Shostakovich: Boosey & Hawkes
George Gershwin: Warner Chappell – Courtesy of Ira and Leonore Gershwin Trusts; used by permission
John Williams: Malcolm Crowthers
Charles Ives: Peermusic Classical – MSS 14, The Charles Ives Papers in the Irving S. Gilmore Music Library of Yale University
Luciano Berio: Universal Edition / Eric Marinitsch
Edgard Varèse: Lebrecht Music & Arts Photo Library
Olivier Messiaen: Malcolm Crowthers
Pierre Boulez: Universal Edition / Eric Marinitsch
Karlheinz Stockhausen: Kathinka Pasveer / Stockhausen.org – Archive of the Stockhausen Foundation for Music, Kuerten
John Cage: Malcolm Crowthers
Steve Reich: Betty Freeman / Lebrecht Music & Arts Photo Library
John Adams: Deborah O'Grady
Arvo Pärt: Universal Edition / Eric Marinitsch
John Tavener: Malcolm Crowthers
Henryk Górecki: Malcolm Crowthers
Sir Harrison Birtwistle: Boosey & Hawkes / Hanya Chlala / Arena PAL
Tōru Takemitsu: Malcolm Crowthers

Index

A

B

M

W

X

Y

Z